THE JESUS DELUSION

THE JESUS DELUSION

ROBERT MACKLIN

BWM Books Pty Ltd
Canberra

Copyright Robert Macklin 2011

Print ISBN 978-0-9876006-6-0

Published by BWM Books Pty Ltd

19 Embling St, Wanniassa

ACT, 2903, Australia

Cover design Ferozidot

This book was produced using PressBooks.com, and PDF rendering was done by PrinceXML.

Dedication

For Rob and Ben

'No one puts new wine into old wineskins.'
Jesus (Mark 2:22)

'Who touched my garments?'
Jesus (Mark 5:30)

'...taking him aside from the multitude privately, he (Jesus) put his fingers into his ears and he spat and touched his tongue; and looking up to heaven he sighed...And his ears were opened, his tongue was released and he spoke plainly.'
(Mark 7:33-35)

'He (Jesus) is possessed by Beelzebub, and by the prince of demons he casts out the demons.'
A Pharisee (Mark 3:22)

'Get behind me, Satan!'
Jesus (to Peter) (Mark 8:33)

'The Son of Man came eating and drinking, and they say, "Behold, a glutton and a drunkard".'
Jesus (Matthew 11:19)

Contents

Introduction ... 1

Part I. The Sources

1. The Setting ... 13
2. The Jews ... 21
3. The Sects ... 29
4. The Writings ... 37

Part II. The Evidence

5. Birth and Childhood ... 59
6. The Family ... 71
7. The Human Figure ... 79
8. Miracles and Healings ... 83
9. The Disciples ... 87

Part III. The Narrative

10. The Man ... 105
11. The Mission ... 121
12. The Messiah ... 139
13. Jerusalem! ... 151
14. Judas ... 167
15. The Last Days ... 179
16. The End ... 191

Epilogue ... 205
Bibiliography ... 209
About the Author ... 213
Acknowledgements ... 215

Introduction

IT is often said that Jesus is the best known person who ever lived. There is undoubtedly an element of truth in the assertion. His name is probably more widely known than any other and a vague outline of his mission and message is familiar to a great segment of humanity.

But of all those who profess knowledge of him, only the slimmest minority, the scholarly few, have anything more than cloudy glimmerings of his life and times. This is just as true among Christians as non-Christians.

Few Christians, for example, know more than the most basic facts concerning Jesus' family and his dealings with them. Most would know the identity of his mother, Miriam (translated as Mary), and Joseph, his legal father. But how many know that he had four brothers – James, Joses, Judas and Simon – and at least two sisters? And of those who were aware of Jesus' family, what proportion would know that his brother James became the leader of the infant Christian Church after Peter and that he himself was executed in Jerusalem in A.D. 62 by a party of Sadducees?[1] How many are aware that relations between Jesus and his family were consistently hostile and are so revealed in every single biblical reference to them? The answer, of course, is only a very small proportion.

There are many other aspects of Jesus' life where ignorance is the rule rather than the exception for Christians and non-Christians alike—his relationships with Judas, John the Baptist, and the Beloved Disciple; his ungovernable temper; his fondness for wine; his decidedly unheroic appearance; and the probable circumstances of his birth. It must be said that in these areas the evidence which will be presented here—much of which contradicts the accepted view—falls short of conclusive proof. All that can be said with certainty is that the conclusions drawn are much more probable than the glossy mythology which has been purveyed for the last two millennia. But the essential point is that in each case ignorance of the facts has been positively encouraged.

The reasons for this are twofold. The first—and morally the more respectable—is the belief of the established Church that Jesus was and is a deity, an equal participant in the three-in-one Godhead which they term the Trinity. Once this is accepted—and in the early Christian centuries the dispute over its acceptance split the Church and was resolved only by fierce politicking and much bloodshed[2]—the human circumstances of Jesus' existence became almost irrelevant. The study of them becomes suspiciously heretical. He is simply the Christ, the only begotten Son of God, who appeared briefly on earth to assure a suffering humanity of God's continuing interest and to offer the Way—the formula—for a blissful life after death.

The other, less commendable reason is the Church's deep concern to present Jesus in the most attractive light possible, to universalise him so that his appeal is as powerful to a Peruvian street child as it is to a millionaire American President. To this end they have highlighted some elements with a fierce intensity—'Suffer the little children'… 'Love your enemies'… —while assigning other equally valid elements—'you brood of vipers'…'I have come to set a man against his father'…[3]—to the shadows of obfuscation and obscurity.

They have, in effect, 'packaged' his personality. They have removed his rantings; they have washed him; they have modelled him by Michelangelo and costumed him by Giotto; they have demotivated and dehumanised him; they have removed him from his time and place; they have moulded him to their will. For their own continuing glorification they have played with truth and turned their plaything into a virtue.

LIVES

Amid the welter of books on Jesus' life over the centuries there have been surprisingly few devoted to the quest for the historical truth of his human circumstances. The reason, of course, is that almost invariably the authors of such books have been convinced Christians and, therefore, prey to the dogma of their times. Non-believers have been discouraged by a variety of means, from execution to simple censorship.

The work of great scholars such as Reimarus, Strauss and Bauer[4] in the 18th and 19th centuries, while invaluable, derived wholly and painstakingly from the received text of the gospels and produced conclusions which to modern eyes seem one-dimensional and unsatisfying. This is not to underrate the importance of their work in any way. Without them, particularly Strauss, it would not be possible to move forward at all. The orthodox, clerical theologians with their vested interest in perpetuating the irrational superstitions and self-contradictory absurdities of traditional Christian belief would have continued their domination of the field.

Strauss and his colleagues make it possible to begin unravelling the life and character of Jesus from certain firm, if modest, intellectual foundations. It can be accepted, for example, that Mark, rather than Matthew, is the prime gospel[5]; that the Greek author of John invented the long, tendentious discourses which he attributed to Jesus (though perhaps the dual nature of the book's authorship has not fully been appreciated); that Jesus' Messiahship can be viewed (and, indeed, even *should* be viewed) within the framework of eschatology, the belief that the end of the world is imminent.

The 20th century, however, did not produce comparable advances among theologians and exegetes. Aside from Albert Schweitzer[6], whose work consolidated and complemented the earlier writers, the best known figures were Rudolf Bultmann, Paul Tillich, and Teilhard de Chardin.[7] None added significantly to the general understanding of the figure at the centre of the Christian religion. And the 21st century, while actively confronting religion itself—most notably in Richard Dawkins' 'The God Delusion' has made few advances in unravelling the mysterious figure of Jesus himself.

The most notable advances have been factual rather than theoretical. The discovery of the Dead Sea Scrolls[8], for example, has provided scholars with an open window into a Jewish sect, the Essenes, which hitherto had been perceived only dimly and at second hand. The idea that the Essenes exerted a powerful influence on the course of Jesus' life was once the province of romantic conspiracy theories among religious novelists. Now, as will be seen, it enters the realm of factual probability.

There is the 1945 discovery in Egypt of a gospel according to Thomas which, alone among gospels, contains a description of Jesus' physical appearance.

There is the immense amount of scholarly work devoted to the biblical text itself. However poetic its rendering, the King James Version has been shown to be inaccurate in very many instances; forgeries and blatant additions have been uncovered and expurgated from the text.

These new tools, combined with the earlier advances and an 'undogmatised' view of the man represent the foundations upon which this present work is built. It is not intended as a definitive Life of Jesus in all its aspects. Rather it is an attempt to cut through the distorted and dishonest picture of Jesus which has accumulated over the centuries. It is a quest for the human truth behind the childish superstitions: the secret life, made so by the passive compliance and active connivance of the Church. It is an effort to present as cogently as possible the evidence which patently contradicts the established view and in so doing come to terms with the reality of the man and his passions.

CHRIST?

The main impediment to gaining an accurate understanding of Jesus the man is the widely held view that he was no man at all but a God in human guise. In fact, so great an emphasis is given to his divinity in the practice (if not theory) of modern Christianity that he now appears to occupy a wholly disproportionate area of the much disputed Trinity. Unquestionably, he overwhelms the Holy Ghost as a significant Trinitarian element. There is even a danger—if danger it really is—that he will so eclipse the Father in the consciousness of the modern believer as to render Him equally irrelevant.

Part of the reason for this development is the tangibility of Jesus. Only a relatively few hard-nosed atheists take the view that he never existed, that his story is no more than the literary invention of an unknown Jewish playwright.[9]

All Christians and the great majority of non-believers are satisfied on the evidence that the man actually existed and that some of his sayings and some of his activities as represented in the gospels actually occurred. An eminently respectable argument has been mounted by the Swedish historian, Alvar Ellegard, that the real Jesus lived at least 100 years earlier than the dates usually ascribed by Christian theologians. Ellegard equates him with the founder of the Essene sect and argues that the 'good news' celebrated by the Apostles Peter and Paul was their several visions of his return as the Christ raised to heaven. In his tightly reasoned work, 'Jesus 100 Years Before Christ' (Overlook Press, 1998) he claims that the four gospels were in effect commissioned and promoted by the early Christian bishop, Ignatius of Antioch, to counter the influence of the Gnostics and others who denied Jesus' humanity and asserted that individuals could worship God directly and without the intercession of a church or clergy.

The argument has much to commend it, but is beyond the intellectual grasp or emotional demands of the Christian laity. The Jesus of tradition dominates the field. And from this tangibility Christian propagandists ('propaganda' being a Christian invention[10]) have been able to spread their message across the face of the earth, tailoring it, as did Peter, 'to the needs of the audience'.[11]

The Father—or to give him his proper name, Yahweh[12]—has not been so easy to 'sell'. He is Jewish in concept and, as revealed in the Old Testament, irascible, vain, secretive, violent, jealous, misogynistic and even misanthropic. In addition, the only time He ever allowed Himself to be seen He presented no more than His 'back parts' for inspection.[13]

Obviously, the Jesus of tradition has had to assume the larger role in the promotion of the religion. But, as has been mentioned, the distorting mirrors of divinity have been scattered around the figure of Jesus to produce a desired effect. And no more powerful or more deceitful an illusion is that provided by the title which so often accompanies his name: Christ.

So prevalent is its use that it has almost taken the form of a divine patronymic. Incorporated into the name of religion itself the word is used to designate not only Jesus' illustrious parentage but his own absolute divinity. It is one of the most striking examples of the Church's misuse of the historical truth. For the word Christ is no more than the anglicisation of the Greek word Christos which is the simple translation of the Hebrew Messiah meaning 'anointed one'. But the essence of the deception lies in the fact that the Anointed One or Messiah had no connotations of divinity. Within the Jewish framework—and thus within Jesus' own consciousness—the awaited Messiah, the one chosen or anointed by Yahweh to bring about the Kingdom of God on earth was as mortal as any other member of the Elect, the people of Israel. It is inconceivable that Jesus or those close to him should have thought otherwise.

The very essence of Judaism is (and has always been) that there be no other god but Yahweh Himself and Jews have demonstrated the intensity of that belief with their lifeblood time without number. The concept of Jesus' divinity arose only when the new religion was forced to adapt itself to pagan attitudes and concepts and only then did the process of deification begin.

That it was facilitated by Jesus' own obsessive need for a spiritual, paternal link with Yahweh cannot be denied. On the contrary, a full realisation of this element of his character is absolutely necessary to a clear understanding of the man. But, as will be seen, this element is illustrative not of his supposed divinity but of his deeply human needs.

JEW?

Jesus' 'Jewishness' is another element which the Christian Church has tried to blot from the picture. In this they are assisted by some of the gospel writers who display fiercely anti-Semitic attitudes. But the fact of Jesus' own perception of himself as a Jew is not really open to argument. The evidence in this case is conclusive. Jesus himself declared it time and again. His assertion that he sought no violence to the established Judaic Law[14]—meaning religious practice—is itself persuasive.

But the final proof lies in the activities of his disciples after his death, the attitudes of those closest to him, those privy to his private thoughts and instruction. As the Acts of the Apostles indicates, they had no desire whatever to take his message to non-Jews. Indeed, such an idea was anathema to them; so much so that when an outsider, Paul, who had never seen or heard Jesus during his lifetime, preached to the Gentiles, the disciples cursed him for it and may well have attempted his assassination.[15] Only when his efforts proved so much more successful—and remunerative—than their own were they prepared to receive him and then only on sufferance.

Quite simply, the course of Jesus' life, his obsessions and his psychological demands can only be viewed within the context of Judaism. Remove him from his time and place and you remove the meat of the man, his emotional raison d'être.

Notes

1. Josephus, Antiquities; Hegesippus, Memoirs (quoted by Eusebius; Church History); Acts 15:13; Galatians 1:18-19.

2. Arias (C A.D. 270-335) a Church father from Alexandria, held the view that Jesus was not wholly divine but had been created ex nihilo by the Father. He was opposed by Athanasius, also an Alexandrian, who held that there had never been a time when Jesus did not exist. The controversy spread through Christendom and the Emperor Constantine was forced to summon an ecumenical Council at Nicaea in A.D. 325. There Arias and his teaching were condemned and the Nicene Creed formulated. However, the dispute continued to rage with first the one side and then the other gaining supremacy at a series of subsequent Councils. The forces of Athanasius were finally victorious though Arianism continued to be taught by heretical groups until the 7th century.

3. Respectively, Matthew 19:14; Matthew 5:44; Matthew 10:352; Matthew 23:33; and Matthew 10:35.

4. Herman Samuel Reimarus, The Aims of Jesus and His Disciples; David Friedrich Strauss, Life of Jesus; Bruno Bauer, Criticism of the Gospel History of John and Thy Synoptics.

5. The mistaken belief that Matthew was the first gospel composed arose from the statement by the early Church father, Papias (C A.D. 144) that, 'Matthew compiled the sayings in the Hebrew language and every man translated them as he was able'. It is now accepted that this could not have referred to the Book of Matthew which was written in Greek. See Chapter 3, 'The Sources'.

6. The Quest of the Historical Jesus, 1911.

7. Rudolf Bultmann, Jesus and the World, The History of the Synoptic Tradition; Paul Tillich, Systematic Theology; Teilhard de Chardin, The Divine Milieu.

8. The group of leather and papyrus manuscripts relating to the group of Essenes who lived in the ancient community of Qumran on the northwestern shore of the Dead Sea. The first of the scrolls was discovered by two shepherd boys in caves near Qumran

in 1947. Subsequent investigations have uncovered more than 500, many fragmentary, but all, in the words of F.M. Cross, former Professor of Hebrew at Harvard, 'throw a brilliant light upon the creative and fluid period before the crystallisation of Jewish and Christian orthodoxy'. See Chapter 3, 'The Sources'.

9. According to this theory, the Jesus Story was an allegorical Passion Play which so affected the epileptic Saul (later Paul) that he found a transcendental truth within it and devoted the rest of his life to spreading its message. See H.W. Smith, Man and His Gods.

10. In the Roman Catholic Church, a committee of cardinals established the Congregation for the Propagation of the Faith (propaganda fide) in 1622.

11. Papias, reported in Eusebias Church History. See p. 37.

12. More strictly YHWH. The name was regarded by the ancient Hebrews as being too sacred to pronounce; thus in the original no vowel signs were used to indicate pronunciation. This led to great confusion among biblical scholars and in the late Middle Ages to a mistranslation as 'Jehovah'. This has now been corrected in all standard texts.

13. Exodus 33:23.

14. Matthew 5:18.

15. Acts 9:23, 11:2; Galatians 2:10.

PART 1

The Sources

1

The Setting

AS a Jew, Jesus shared with his fellow religionists an extraordinary past. What little is known of their early history has come down chiefly through the stories of the Old Testament, in most cases written long after the events they describe. But two crucial facts lie at the basis of it all. The first is the geographical location of Palestine, the homeland of the Jews since about the 18th century B.C., sandwiched as it was between the great Empires of the Euphrates-Tigris basin in the north and the Nile in the south. The second is their concept of themselves as the Chosen People, the Elect of Yahweh the one true God.

While there can be no certainty, it is generally accepted by historians that Abraham led his people from Ur, a state in Mesopotamia, to Palestine about 3,800 years ago and there they gradually gave up their nomadic ways and settled in family groups. One family, headed by Jacob (or Israel) found its way south into territory dominated by the kings of Egypt and when next they are heard from are oppressed and enslaved by the Pharaoh. Of those who remained in Palestine, some continued their covenant with Yahweh—the chief rite of which was circumcision—while some adopted other local deities.

At an unknown date, Moses arose as a leader of the 'Israelites' in the south and began a mass movement which has as its only historical parallel the Long March of the Chinese under Mao Zedong. In the course of the migration, Moses established a new covenant with Yahweh—the Ten Commandments—and led his people north into Palestine. Prior to Mount Sinai, Yahweh had been little more than a war god, a spiritual protector dispensing and withholding favours at will. But by the introduction of moral strictures a new dimension was added to the Godhead, and, incidentally, to the authority of his servant, Moses—a useful attribute for any leader charged with the well-being and good order of a mass migration on such a scale.

As is well known, Moses did not reach the Promised Land himself. After forty years of wandering in the wilderness (apparently he chose a circuitous route) Moses died and it fell to his successor, Joshua, to conquer the cities and towns of settled Palestine and establish a *Lebensraum* for his people.

A priestly line had been established through Moses' brother, Aaron, and it fell to them to promulgate the Yahwist religion in the 'new' land. They were not successful and the so-called nation of Israel was dissipated into small and often antagonistic communities. This allowed the rise of a rival group, the Philistines, who divided and conquered the Jews, stole the Ark of the Covenant[1] from the temple in Shilo, the then capital in the north and established themselves as rulers of the region. This in turn had the effect of reuniting the people in common enmity and under the warrior-king Saul they struggled to regain their dominant position.

Saul was only partially successful. Though history is not very clear on this point, it seems that Saul had a rival in the priest/prophet Samuel. The people apparently looked to Samuel for the spiritual authority which the rough soldier Saul could not provide and the division of loyalties prohibited a concerted deployment of their forces. When Saul died the Philistines still held sway.

It fell to the most heroic of all Jewish kings, David, to achieve a final and decisive victory. In about 1000 B.C. he routed the Philistines, captured Jerusalem in the south and established it as the Jewish capital. He recaptured the Ark of the Covenant and placed it in a temple there. The focus of Jewish religious activity suddenly shifted from north to south, a move which would have consequences for all of Jewish history and beyond—for the division between north and south would always remain, and its effects would still be felt by the man Jesus 1,000 years later.

David gave Samuel a position of high status at court and in so doing re-established the tradition of spiritual leadership within the processes of government. His son Solomon retained the practice and in his reign Palestine enjoyed its first golden age. As the country prospered he was able to build the great Temple which would become the central symbol of Judaism in the years to come.

But with prosperity came ennui among the people and temptation to the rival powers both without and within. After Solomon's death the Egyptians invaded and though they permitted freedom of worship, the power of the state was broken. Petty kingdoms were established; seizing their opportunity, the Philistines again entered the lists in a long drawn-out struggle for supremacy.

Another Jewish king, Omri, arose and reunited the people. The war they fought was not only for temporal power but for the supremacy of Yahweh over the rival nature-God, Baal.[2] With the assistance of the heroic and legendary prophet, Elijah, they were victorious.

But again the pendulum swung, leadership faded and the governance of the nation bordered on anarchy. In this time, 850-750 B.C., there developed a line of prophets beginning with Amos and Hosea and continuing to Isaiah, Micah, and beyond. The effect of their teaching was all-important in the development of Jewish religious consciousness. Like Moses they too added to the concept of Yahweh, investing Him with universality and a love of 'righteousness' and, in the case of Isaiah, a vision of His chosen people as the Suffering Servants of God who would one day reap a mighty reward—spiritual dominion over all the nations of the earth.

Also at this time the land was officially divided into two kingdoms, Israel in the north and Judah (later Judea) in the south. The boundaries were shattered as Assyria invaded from the north and demanded tribute and slaves but were re-established as the Assyrian Empire decayed. But then a resurgent Egypt made its own demands and statecraft and diplomacy became an all-consuming preoccupation for both lay[3] and religious leaders alike. Throughout, the Jewish religion was maintained and even strengthened by the presence of the oppressors.

With the fall of Assyria a new power arose in the east: the Babylonians (or Chaldeans) were on the march. The northern kingdom remained clear of the fray but Judah sided with Egypt and resisted the Babylonian encroachment. Finally, Nebuchadnezzar laid siege to Jerusalem. For eighteen months the Judeans waited in vain for the promised Egyptian reinforcements and in one of the more decisive moments of history, their city fell in 586 B.C. Many thousands of Jews were carried off to Babylon while many more fled to Egypt. Jerusalem was burned, and the great Temple of Solomon was destroyed.

Little is known of the course of events for the next fifty years in either Babylon or Palestine. But in 538 B.C. Cyrus, founder of the Persian Empire, took Babylon and became convinced that the Temple must be rebuilt. His decision remains a mystery.[4] But whatever the reason (and the majority of Jews saw it as a miraculous intervention from Yahweh) the exiles slowly made their way back to Palestine where in most cases their land had been appropriated by those fortunate enough to have remained behind.

Nominally, power in the state remained in the hands of the Persians but in Jerusalem the High Priest exercised the powers of a king with priests and nobles as his departmental ministers. This form of government—a forerunner of the Sanhedrin—would be maintained for at least three hundred years and even when supplanted by foreign conquest would retain great authority over the mass of the Jewish people.

Two other vitally important elements returned from Babylon with the exiles. One was the prophet Ezra who re-organised the priesthood and consolidated its power as a ruling class. He also demanded of the people recognition of their exclusivity as the Chosen of God. Intermarriage with members of other religions was severely discouraged and even banned outright. Jews were forced to turn away from the world and to rediscover their own uniqueness.

The second, even more far-reaching element was the notion of the Saviour or Messiah chosen by God to lead his people to deliverance. It was a Persian concept but it quickly gained favour among a people whose entire history must have seemed tailor-made for it: an oppressed people exchanging one overlord for another, one national tragedy for the next and for as long as anyone could know. Surely all this suffering could not have been in vain; surely the hand of Yahweh was discernible behind it, testing his chosen ones in the crucible of pain and despair until they were fitted to become his 'kingdom of priests and a holy nation'?[5] Obviously, the Messiah would be the one chosen by Yahweh to herald that great moment.

It was also a time of great literary activity. The Old Testament appears to have found its final form during this period. A great deal of apocalyptic and prophetic literature appeared, books such as Enoch and Daniel which were, by their nature, subject to all kinds of interpretation.

This was equally true of the concept of the Messiah which took a number of different forms among various religious sects. But all shared two common elements. The first was that a leader would arise from within Israel[6], who would herald the end of the world in its present form. It would be replaced by a world from which all evil would be cast out so that justice—and the priestly supremacy of Israel—would prevail forever.

The second element was a belief that the Messiah would appear at the End of the Days—the Last Times which would be characterised by the most terrible catastrophes: drought, plagues, foreign invasion, blasphemy and slaughter among the Elect. From the time of these horrors the Messiah would arise and call upon Israel to repent its sins and reunite itself with Yahweh, the one true God. When that was achieved—and only then—would God re-establish the heaven upon earth which had been lost so long ago in the tragedy of Eden.

It should, however, be understood that messianism at that time did not enthrall the whole nation. It was more in the nature of a growing cult and while its adherents came from all levels of society, the intensity of their commitment varied greatly. Not unnaturally, the most enthusiastic followers were the group with the least to lose in the present order: the poor, the weak, and the physically and emotionally crippled. The Establishment, more often than not, preferred the status quo.

One calculation taken from Daniel which would gain wide acceptance was that the Last Times would begin 490 years from the time of Cyrus' command to rebuild the Temple.[7] If this were true and accurate, the Last Times could be expected to begin around 48 B.C. and the Messiah would arise some time after that. But that was looking far into the future. No one could know that by that time the necessary conditions would seem to so many—and to one man in particular—to have been fulfilled to the letter.

Notes

1. Believed to be a rectangular timber box perhaps two metres long by one metre wide by one metre deep, inlaid with semi-precious stones and surmounted by two large cherubim. An early tradition has it that the Ark was carried through the wilderness by Moses and the Israelites, perhaps containing the two stone tablets on which the Ten Commandments were carved.
2. Baal was symbolised by a phallic stone plinth and was venerated as the 'husband' of the land. His best known follower is the temptress Jezebel.
3. The Egyptians 'farmed' their tax-gathering operation among prominent members of the Jewish lay community. The chief tax farmer became highly influential and on occasion sought to supplant the High Priest in the government of the country.
4. The Royal Household of Judea were among the exiles in Babylon. The most likely explanation is that Cyrus was influenced by their cooperation during and after the fall of the city.
5. Exodus 19:6.
6. Hebrew: 'Contender with God'. The term is used to designate both the ancient northern state of Palestine and collectively the members of the Jewish religious community.
7. Daniel 9:24-27.

2

The Jews

WHEN Alexander the Great began his advance on Egypt from his conquest of Asia Minor in 333 B.C. the religious hierarchy of Jerusalem was waiting for him and was well-prepared. The High Priest met the conqueror at the frontier of Palestine and surrendered before a blow was struck. In return, Alexander permitted the Jews to continue as a semi-autonomous state, their only real obligation to the Emperor being a hefty annual tribute from the Temple treasury.

When Alexander died in 323 B.C., however, the balance of power in the civilised world changed swiftly and his appointees and their successors in the various provinces quickly sought to consolidate their own power. In 320 B.C. the Greek overlord of Egypt, Ptolemy, captured Judea in a single day, a Sabbath when the Jews were not prepared to break scripture even to the extent of defending themselves against an invader. But as was the Egyptian practice, freedom of worship was again permitted within the vassal state.

This relatively acceptable status was suddenly lost when in 198 B.C. the Greek Selucids, heirs to Alexander's eastern empire, defeated the Egyptians and imposed their much stricter controls. They established satrapies and appointed rulers whose Hellenistic outlook coincided with their own. To such men—often highly civilised and Athenian educated—the oriental barbarism of the Jews with their joyless quest for 'righteousness' and their moral despotism was distasteful in the extreme. To the pious Jews the cultivated beauty of Greek civilisation with its sensuous architecture and dress, its secular education system, and its pride and delight in the human form was an abomination, a blasphemy in the eyes of the Lord.

Co-existence was impossible; and the situation worsened as the Selucids came to realise the strategic importance of the buffer state between themselves and the Egyptians. To protect their flanks they embarked on a policy which would transform Palestine into a Greek outpost, a homogeneous portion of their dominions.

The situation was complicated by the fact that many of the Jewish aristocracy, including members of the priestly class, welcomed the new, more tolerant way of life. Thus Onias III was ousted as High Priest by his brother Jason[1] who was more amenable to the Empire's demands. Jason in turn was replaced by other High Priests even more willing to accept Grecian ideals.

But even that was insufficient for the Selucid king, Antiochus IV Epiphanes. First he installed a Greek garrison in Jerusalem and then on his return from an unsuccessful foray into Egyptian territory, occupied the city and despoiled the Temple. He greatly enlarged the garrison, placed a new (foreign) governor in charge of Judea and set about his mission to destroy Judaism by incorporating it into the all-embracing Grecian pantheon. To the horror of the Jews he identified Yahweh with Zeus and erected a statue to the god in the Temple itself.[2] Similar shrines were established in many provincial cities. The practice of circumcision was banned as was the Sabbath observance so beloved of the Jews.

It was the final blasphemy, 'the abomination of desolation',[3] and open rebellion flared when a provincial priest, Mattathias of the House of Hasmon, murdered a fellow Jew as he prepared to worship at the foreign altar. Mattathias immediately took refuge in the surrounding hills and under the leadership of his eldest son, Judas (known as the Maccabee), the Jewish rebels harassed the Selucid forces in a classic campaign of guerrilla warfare.

Judas was fortunate in that other parts of the empire were also rebelling, particularly the Parthians in the east, and Antiochus was suddenly defending his territory on many fronts. Nevertheless, Judas was an outstanding general and in 165 B.C. his forces occupied Jerusalem and 'cleansed' the Temple.

For the next thirty years Judas and his brothers fought to maintain the 'purity' of Judaism in the country and to a great degree they were successful. But the purely religious motives of the rebellion were gradually expanded to include a quest for national independence. The Greek garrison was finally forced out of Jerusalem and in 140 B.C. Simon, Judas' brother, became High Priest, Prince and Military Commander, all titles to be hereditary henceforth. By now the 'purity' of the Hasmonean quest for a religious state had long since dissipated.

After Simon's murder (by his son-in-law, the Governor of Jericho) in 135 B.C., his son, John Hyrcanus I assumed the throne and almost immediately became embroiled in the final attempt by the Selucids to reassert their authority over Judea. When the invasion failed—due mainly to the emergence of a new force in the region, the Romans—John Hyrcanus set about consolidating the principality. He attacked the neighbouring Idumaeans and forced them to adopt Judaism. He routed the Samaritans and destroyed their Temple (to Yahweh) on Mount Gerizim. When he died in 105 B.C. his son, Judas Aristobulus, formally adopted the title of King.

Judas Aristobulus was succeeded by another of John Hyrcanus' sons, Alexander Jannaeus, whose reign was filled with bloodshed, anarchy and rebellion. His death in 76 B.C. was the closing act in the era of Jewish independence. The time had almost come for Imperial Rome to take its place in the long line of Jewish overlords. The widow of Alexander Jannaeus, Salome Alexandra, tried to placate the contending forces both within the country and on its borders but the task was beyond her. When she died in 67 B.C. a war of accession developed between her sons Hyrcanus II and Aristobulus II.

Both parties submitted their claims to the Roman general, Pompey, whose legions had just conquered Damascus, and in 63 B.C. he decided for Hyrcanus. Aristobulus gathered his armies in Jerusalem and fortified the city against an expected siege. Pompey advanced on the city and slowly forced the defenders back until only the Temple remained and there they held out for three long months. When the last defences were breached, 12,000 Jews were put to the sword and hundreds more leapt to their deaths from the high walls.

The whole of Judea became part of the Roman province of Syria with Hyrcanus as High Priest but subservient to Antipater, an Idumaean leader who had thrown his forces into the struggle in support of Pompey. Once again the Jews were in chains.

The only consolation offered to the faithful was Pompey's gesture in allowing them to retain the Temple treasure, though he did exact a large tribute in gold before he left for Rome. Even that was lost nine years later when another Roman leader, Marcus Licinius Crassus, a Governor of Syria, plundered the Temple of 10,000 talents before meeting his death in battle at Ctesiphon.

After the years of relative freedom the Jews chafed in the Roman shackles and armed rebel bands began to appear in the north. Roman retribution was swift— 30,000 Jews were sold into slavery.

Then in 43 B.C. the Idumaean, Antipater, was poisoned[4], and the Parthians invaded Judea and placed their own puppet sovereign on the provincial throne. The Romans, Mark Anthony and Octavian responded by declaring Herod, the son of Antipater, the rightful king of the Jews. With Roman backing and a Jewish army Herod took the throne and then the nation by force in 37 B.C.

Herod ruled for thirty-three tempestuous years. In any other kingdom he might have been judged a remarkable success. He played politics on the international stage and became known by his contemporaries as Herod the Great. He extended the nation's frontiers. He erected magnificent public buildings and rebuilt whole cities investing them with the voluptuous beauty of Greek architecture. He encouraged the arts. He was a patron of the Olympic Games.[5] He rebuilt and extended the sacred Temple and even professed himself a Jew. Yet in Israel he was detested with a terrible passion.

No one believed his protestations of Jewish conversion and in this they were correct. It was no more than a political ploy and a half-hearted one at that. Their gratitude for the rebuilt Temple turned to disgust when he unveiled the golden eagle—a graven image and symbol of the hated Roman oppressors—at the very entrance to the shrine.

The stylish Hellenistic buildings and cities were seen by the pious as decadent and the naked statues displayed there were thought to be almost as revolting as the naked athletes who competed in his Games and Festivals. Commerce was corrupting, usury a sin.

The king's private morals were just as reprehensible as his public decadence. He took a total of ten wives and within the court his excesses were legion. He became obsessed by the idea that members of his family were plotting his death; and his suspicions were well-founded. But the drowning of his son and the murder of his wife Marianne (among others) only confirmed for the Jews their belief that the alien Idumaean was an instrument of the devil.

The earth itself confirmed their judgement. In the seventh year of his reign a great earthquake killed hundreds of the faithful[6]; persistent drought blighted the land; and in the fourteenth year a plague of locusts swept over the countryside and levelled the crops. In a land of 2,500,000 people, most dependent on farming for their livelihood, these were tragedies of the first magnitude.

Time and again plans were laid by groups of activists to assassinate the alien. On every occasion they were discovered by Herod's spies and his vengeance was swift. When he died, aged sixty-nine, of dropsy, ulcers, fever and convulsions in 4 B.C., the people first rejoiced and then armed themselves for rebellion against his successors.

Under the terms of his will the kingdom was divided among three of his sons: Herod Antipas, who received the northern province of Galilee and an area east of the Jordan known as Peraea; Archelaus, who took Judea which included the southern cities of Bethlehem, Caesarea, Emmaus and the capital Jerusalem; and Philip, who governed Batanea to the east of the Sea of Galilee.

The first skirmish between nationalist Jews and the new kings broke out in Jerusalem almost immediately. During the Passover of 4 B.C., Archelaus and a force of Roman troops slew 3,000 insurrectionists and put the revolt down, temporarily at least. But at the very next religious feast—the Pentecost—resistance erupted again and once more the rebels were slaughtered.

In the countryside rebel bands attacked Roman supporters and at times invaded towns and cities which had shown themselves sympathetic to the hated aliens. The most spectacular was the capture of Sepphoris, the capital of Galilee, by the patriot leader Judas of Gamala[7] in A.D. 6-7. Once again the might of Rome crushed the incipient rebellion. Varus, the

Governor of Syria, marched through Galilee razing hundreds of towns and villages with his 20,000 soldiers; a rampage which ended with the crucifixion of 2,000 rebels and a further 30,000 Jews sold into slavery.

North and south the country was ablaze; families mourned for sons and daughters killed in battle, raped, or sold to the highest bidder at auction. Crops withered on the vine or in the fields and those that were harvested were appropriated by the invaders. Reinforcements from Rome established garrisons throughout the country with the heaviest concentration on the most troublesome of all provinces: the traditional seat of rebellion, Galilee.

To the messianists throughout Israel the evidence was inescapable: the age of the End of the Days, the Last Times, had begun. If the Messiah were ever to appear, now, surely, was the time.

Notes

1. The name itself is a strong indication of the extent to which Hellenisation had penetrated the Jewish aristocracy.
2. Its face bore a strong resemblance to Antiochus himself. As in most historical references in this chapter, the principal authority is Josephus.
3. Daniel 12:11.
4. Probably by his son, Herod.
5. Without Herod's financial support the Olympic Games of 12 B.C. would not have been able to proceed. In recognition he was made President of the Games, a position never held before or since.
6. The Dead Sea Scrolls indicate that it also badly damaged the monastic settlement at Qumran.
7. Also known as Judas of Galilee, his rallying cry was, 'No ruler but God'. Inevitably, he was acclaimed by some as the Messiah.

3

The Sects

AMONG the Jews, three major sects controlled the religious life of the people. All contained elements who believed implicitly in the imminent arrival of the Messiah, though their vision of the kind of man he would be differed widely. However, it should be stressed that none thought of him as being other than a perfectly mortal human.

The *Sadducees* were an aristocratic, priestly class whose members usually controlled the Temple's finances and who grew rich in the service of Yahweh. They were naturally the most politically conservative of the sects, the least affected by messianism, and most co-operative to the Roman overlords.

They preached a strict and literal adherence to the Law of Moses and the cultivation of a severe code of ethics. Those among them who adhered to the cult believed that if a Messiah were to arise he would come from their own class and share their views. He would be a new Moses, combining temporal and priestly power and by the force of his will and his law deliver his people from bondage.[1]

The *Pharisees* were a divided sect with some following the precepts of Hillel[2], a gentle soul who lived in the 1st century B.C. and whose teaching often parallels the more attractive features of Jesus' own message. Others were followers of the conservative Shammai and were much stricter in their interpretation of the Law. In their eyes righteousness became synonymous with ritual.

As a group, the Pharisees regarded Roman oppression almost as inevitable, a cross to be borne on earth for the hope of immortality beyond the grave. In their pastoral work they wielded great influence over the people. They interpreted the Law to cover nearly every aspect of daily life and in general they set an example of the manner in which a pious Jew should conduct himself. They lived simply, condemned luxury, fasted frequently and washed ritually. They were often in conflict with the Sadducees over the spiritual significance of some particular law but joined with them in the great council of the church, the Sanhedrin, to administer the spiritual affairs of the nation.

To messianic Pharisees, when the saviour of Israel arose he would be another David: a king marching at the head of a great army of the faithful, a charismatic leader who would unite all the people under his banner and with the force of righteousness behind him, drive every last Gentile from the Holy Land.

(The Scribes, often mentioned in conjunction with the Pharisees in the gospels, were not a sect but a profession. They were trained exponents and teachers of the Law and were employed by both Sadducees and Pharisees to draft updated versions of Mosaic Law which by change of custom—particularly in commercial transactions, inheritance and purification rituals—had become outmoded.)

The Essenes saw themselves as the Saints of the Elect, a monastic religious order whose importance to the development of the Christian message was unappreciated until the discovery of the Dead Sea Scrolls. They usually lived in closed communities in the western and northern region of Palestine and within the commune they tilled the soil, ate at a common table and elected their leaders. In the Community Rule from the Dead Sea Scrolls relating to Qumran, it is said: 'They (the leaders) shall preserve the faith in the land with steadfastness and meekness and atone for sin by practice of justice and by suffering the sorrows of afflictions... and they shall be an agreeable offering, atoning for the land and determining the judgement of wickedness, and there shall be no more iniquity.'

The similarities between the Essenes' Community Rule and elements of Jesus' own message are striking. They believed passionately that a Messiah would arise in the land and that he would usher in a Kingdom of Heaven on earth. They agreed with other sects that this would only happen after the Elect had repented their sins. But they despaired of this ever happening if the Elect included all the people of Israel. Accordingly, they refined the concept to an elect of the Elect and, not unnaturally, identified themselves as the group in question.

Sometimes individual members left the group and lived in the towns but even there they separated themselves from the rest of the community. They were ardent pacifists and devoted believers in a version of the oral and written law of Israel. If they married they were enjoined to restrict their sex life to a joyless quest for children and they were similarly ascetic in their other personal habits. Like most people of the time they believed that disease was caused by evil spirits and were convinced of the existence of both angels and demons. They doted on a forthcoming battle between the forces each represented.

They were greatly influenced by the apocalyptic literature, books such as Daniel, Jonah and Enoch, only the first of which has been canonised in the Old Testament and then only a bowdlerised version.

Through the discovery of the Scrolls there is now evidence to support the view that Jesus' brother James was at one time, if not throughout his adult life, a member of the sect. James practised the Law in all its severity, ate no meat, drank no wine, had only one garment and never cut his hair or beard. In the New Testament letter ascribed to him he mentions his illustrious brother only in passing but hammers home the message of virtuous asceticism so beloved of the Essenes. In the letter of Jude, another brother of Jesus, the book of Enoch is quoted as the principal authority for his warning to beware of 'ungodly persons' seeking to 'pervert the grace of our God into licentiousness'.[3]

There is no record in the gospels of any relationship between Jesus himself and the Essenes, though there can be little doubt that he was aware of their teaching. This is in stark contrast to both the Pharisees and the Sadducees with whom he was often in conflict. The absence of any specific reference to the Essenes is itself significant, particularly in view of the strong possibility that at least one of his brothers was, if not an active member, certainly a supporter of their attitudes.

It is significant, too, that the phrase Son of Man which Jesus used habitually to describe himself is an Essenean term, one which they applied to themselves collectively. It is a short step to reduce its meaning to apply to a single human being. Similarly, it requires only a single conceptual jump to refine the concept of the elect of the Elect from a group of Saints to one individual who 'shall be an agreeable offering atoning for the land'.

The Essenes believed that the Messiah would be a priestly figure, a teacher of righteousness as opposed to the Davidic warrior of the Pharisees or the Mosaic patriarch of the Sadducees.[4] Like the other sects they also believed that he would come from their own ranks.

A fourth sect, less important to the Jewish people as a whole but with particular significance to Jesus, was that of the *Zealots*. They were activists, deeply patriotic and motivated by zeal for the Torah[5], and like the Pharisees and Sadducees, they were a political party as well as a religious order. They were active in both Jerusalem, where they regarded it as their duty to assassinate any Roman who dared enter the consecrated area of the Temple; and Galilee, where they supported Judas of Gamala in the revolt of A.D. 6-7. Their Messiah would likewise be an activist himself, a revolutionary who would not rest until the hated invaders were driven out.

The Zealots refused to pay taxes and harassed the Roman administration at every opportunity. From the beginning of the Christian era their influence grew and during the great revolt of A.D. 66 they attracted followers from all social classes.

The influence of all major sects was felt in the Galilee of the time and it is not easy, from so great a distance, to gauge their effect on the community in which Jesus' own views were developed. Moreover, they were certainly not the only messianic sects exerting an influence. In addition there were Mandaeans, Galileans, Masbutheans, and Samaritans who were opposed to the Judean traditions believing that the southerners had falsified the Law of Moses.

Indeed, an appreciation of this antagonism between northern (Galilean) and southern (Judean) Palestine is vital in understanding not only the development of Jesus' teaching but the response to his mission by Judeans and the subsequent development of Christianity.

In addition to the historic divisions between them, the northerners spoke a more guttural form of Aramaic than their southern brethren and were not easily understood in the south. For this reason and because of their reputation for fiery politico-religious zeal, the more sophisticated southerners looked askance at their country cousins. For their part, the northerners often referred to Judeans as Jews to differentiate the southerners from themselves. It was not a term of endearment though it lacked the overtones of hysteria with which later Christian exponents infused into it.

But the division was there and it meant that the views of the Sadducees, the aristocratic southern party, were not as popular in the north; the views of the Pharisees who wooed the middle class were also less effective there than in the south. The Essenes in the communes were not active 'fishers of men' in the Christian sense and other sects were often based on tribal or clannish criteria and relished their exclusivity.

Of course, in the political conditions of the time this exclusiveness broke down as groups were forced to cooperate with each other against the oppressive power of Rome and the Hellenising blasphemy of Herod. This brought about a vigorous exchange of views among them and the inevitable distribution of elements from one or other among the rest. It also had the effect of increasing the intensity of the expectation among all the sects and, through them, the common people of the towns and countryside.

But it must be remembered that though the messianic hope was far and away the most important, it was only one of the preoccupations of the people both north and south. Magic and witchcraft flourished. Thaumaturgists—miracle workers—toured the provinces with their bands of assistants. Astrologers catered to both highborn and lowly. Faith healers exorcised demons from the demented. An entire nation was gripped by a spiritual fever which would only be relieved by a total war on the oppressor, a blood-letting as terrible as anything the people of Israel had suffered in all their beleaguered history.

But that fearful slaughter would not come until A.D. 66 and by then the man who had believed himself to be their Messiah and who had revealed his identity to them had been dead in an unmarked pauper's grave for at least thirty years.

Notes

1. It is significant that though there were messianists among the Sadducees, the sect did not believe in an after-life. For them, as for others, the New Kingdom to be established by the messiah would be quite earthbound.
2. The apostle Paul claimed that Gamaliel, grandson of Hillel, who reputedly succeeded his grandfather as High Priest, had been his (Paul's) religious instructor.
3. Jude 1:4-16.
4. However, it should be noted that theirs was a fluid conception and from the Dead Sea Scrolls it can be deduced that not one but two Messiahs were expected.
5. The whole body of Jewish literature including the Scriptures, the Talmud etc.

4

The Writings

THE prime sources of information on the life of Jesus are, of course, the four canonised gospels: Mark, Matthew, Luke and John. The gospels are dealt with in this order throughout since this is the sequence in which they were written.

As will be seen, the authority of all four is uncertain, though there is some evidence to suggest that Mark actually wrote the book which bears his name and that the author of the fourth gospel was named John, though he was certainly not the disciple of the same name.

With Matthew and Luke it is virtually certain that the unknown authors took the names of the disciple and the apostle respectively and may have been followers of them. It is also likely that in each case they used material written much earlier than their books. These documents, known as 'Q'—which may have been a collection of Jesus' sayings—and the Logia—which drew upon Old Testament texts in an attempt to show that Jesus was the Messiah who had been foretold there—are lost. Their former existence has simply been postulated by scholars from internal evidence in the gospels and by reference in much later works. It seems, too, that Mark was aware of the Logia but chose not to rely on it to legitimise Jesus' claims.

None of the gospels was written in Palestine. On the evidence, the likelihood is that Mark was written in Italy, Matthew in Alexandria (Egypt), Luke in Greece and John in Asia Minor. All four were written long after the traditional death of Jesus which is believed to have occurred in A.D. 36. The earliest, Mark, was composed after A.D. 70 and the latest, John, after 115.[1]

The dating of the books is important for two reasons. The obvious one is the availability of eyewitnesses to the events they describe. Clearly, by the time Mark began his writing any living eyewitnesses would have been aged, their memories suspect and at least tinted by the embellishment to which all men are subject when describing the most important period of their lives. By the time Matthew was composed after A.D. 95 the author was forced to rely on second- and third-hand sources, the most important being the book of Mark itself. The same applies to Luke which was published after A.D. 105. John is a special case, but equally the distance in time from the events described therein is so great that like the others it can be relied upon only to provide clues to the total story of Jesus' life.

The second reason is less well appreciated. All were written after the great uprising of the Jews against Rome in A.D. 66 which culminated in the destruction of the Temple in Jerusalem in A.D. 70. It was a ruthless and terrible war. In the siege of Jerusalem alone, with its population swelled by pilgrims and refugees from the countryside, more than a million people are believed to have perished. In Galilee, the most violent province, towns and villages were laid waste in a purge which, according to the historian (and participant) Josephus, turned the Sea of Galilee red with blood and littered its shores with wrecks and swollen corpses.

At the beginning of the uprising, the Romans and other Gentiles of Caesarea massacred 20,000 Jews in the city and similar barbarities decimated the Jewish population across the whole northern section of Palestine, the homeland of Jesus.

The spiritual effect of the war on nascent Christianity was far-reaching, but the purely physical effect was devastating.

Written records and the remaining eyewitnesses alike were destroyed, crushed beneath the iron heel of colonial Rome.

It is a feature of Jewish history that its most terrible tragedies have resulted in its most influential literature. Perhaps this latest destruction was the spur which impelled Mark to write his gospel, but it did mean that suddenly—despite the fact that the nascent Christian community tried very hard to stay out of the war—the resources which he and the other gospel writers could call upon were meagre and unreliable.

Beyond the gospels, the sources available include the works of Josephus[2] who wrote at the end of the first and the beginning of the second centuries A.D. Josephus was born in Jerusalem in A.D. 38 of aristocratic parents. He was a brilliant and wilful young man and at one stage ran away from home to follow a religious figure named Bannus who, like John the Baptist, roamed the wilderness. He returned after three years, became a Pharisee and led a band of rebels in Galilee during the war against Rome.

Josephus defended the stronghold of Jotapata against a Roman siege led by Vespasian until only forty of his men remained alive, hidden in a cave. Josephus decided the time had come for surrender but his fanatical cohorts disagreed and threatened to kill him if he did so. Since they preferred death to surrender he persuaded them to draw lots to determine the order in which each should die at the hand of his brother-at-arms. When only one remained Josephus convinced him of the futility of death and they both surrendered.

At the point of being shipped to Rome in chains Josephus prophesied that his conqueror, Vespasian, would soon become Emperor of Rome; impressed by Josephus' perspicacity, Vespasian released him. Josephus changed sides in the war and soon became a trusted adviser to the Roman, though he was hated by the Jews forever afterwards.

After the fall of Jerusalem he went to Rome and under the direct patronage of Vespasian's son, Titus, wrote some of the most valuable books in all of literature. Without them the circumstances surrounding the life and times of Jesus would be lost to modern scholarship.

In his works Josephus mentions Jesus not at all. The disparaging reference to 'the so-called Christ'[3] and a second claiming divinity for Jesus are universally accepted by scholars as blatant forgeries.

Other sources include the Dead Sea Scrolls, the Talmud, the Koran and the writings of early Church fathers such as Papias and Eusebius. Besides Josephus, secular sources include references from Tacitus[4] and Pliny the Younger[5]. But altogether these are useful only in providing a framework. Without them the inconsistencies and outright contradictions of the gospels would make Jesus' life incomprehensible to one seeking its essential truth. With them we are able to form a picture of the man and his times, to understand his worth and to appreciate his message.

An additional source, which I have used only circumspectly, is the New Testament Apocrypha, the many gospels and acts under the names of Peter, Philip, Thomas, Nicodemus, Barnabas and others which purport to record aspects of Jesus' life and teaching as well as adventures of the apostles in strange, mystical kingdoms. Most are well-meaning and in some cases sound at least as authentic as parts of Matthew, Luke and John. But when the final decision on the composition of the New Testament was taken by a Church Council in Rome in A.D. 382 those then extant (and which were brought to the attention of the Council) were excluded. Their value is marginal. They throw light on certain aspects of Jesus' life which are mentioned only in passing in the canonised gospels.

Essentially, it is the gospels to which one must turn to find the separate pieces which together form the half-completed puzzle. And it must be remembered that in doing so—in addition to all the other impediments to clarity—the earliest manuscripts available only go back to A.D. 350. Thus from the time they were first composed, the gospels passed through the hands of many copyists and translators, all of whom could, and probably did, change and censor the material to fit their own spiritual, apologetic and egotistic ends.

It must also be noted that the gospels are by no means the first New Testament writings still extant. Pride of place must go to the evangelist Paul, whose voluminous letters to his congregations preaching in Jesus' name take up nearly half the space in the Bible of all four gospels combined.

Paul began to write at least thirty years before the first gospel was composed, yet in the whole of his work we find barely a reference to the human circumstances of Jesus' life and only the vaguest allusions to his teachings. The stories and parables and sayings which occupy the greater part of Matthew and Luke are conspicuous by their absence. Indeed, Paul seems to actively discourage his readers from delving into that world at all. His whole concentration is upon the metaphysical concept of Jesus as the Son of God, the divinity resurrected. Of Jesus' essentially human life he cares not a jot and this is curious. If Jesus was a contemporary, or if he led a blameless life, why suppress it? If Paul knew the facts of Jesus' life from his long association with the disciples—his parentage; the circumstances of his boyhood and youth; his effect upon the crowds who came to hear him speak; his messianic conviction; the drama of his trial and death – he speaks barely a word of them to congregations starved of such information.[6]

This is clearly the action of a man with a fixed idea, a singular obsession, who will not allow his concept to be tarnished by reality. It was a reality which, if we accept the traditional Jesus figure of the gospels, would have undermined the perfection of his concept. It would have rooted the feet of his deity firmly in the earth of Galilee and Judea, and to Paul—as to many present-day Christians—the idea was unconscionable.

Fortunately, the gospels are not so attenuated—though all suffer from the same syndrome to some degree—and it is to them that we must turn.

MARK

We do not know who Mark was. Someone of that name may well have written the gospel. There is a Christian tradition that he was a leader of the Alexandrian church, another that he was the son of Peter.[7] But when a Mark is mentioned in the Acts of the Apostles, it is as a companion of Paul on his evangelical travels and in the early Church Paul and Peter were on opposing sides of a doctrinal schism. Paul was convinced that he must take his message to the Gentiles while Peter and James led 'the circumcision party'[8] which held that only Jews should be admitted to the Church.

The early – and thoroughly unreliable – Church father, Papias[9], wrote in about A.D. 144:

> Mark, having become the interpreter of Peter, set down accurately as much as he remembered—though not in order—of the things said and done by Christ. For neither did he hear the Lord, nor did he follow him; but afterwards, as I said, followed Peter who adapted his instructions to the needs (of his audience) but had no design to provide a connected account of the things relating to the Lord. So then Mark made no mistake in setting down some things as he

remembered them; for he took care not to omit anything he heard or to include anything false.

Despite the schism in the ranks it is possible, but unlikely, that Mark did attend both Peter and Paul, serving as the fisherman's interpreter (from Aramaic to Greek) until the old man's death, and then joining up with Paul on his much longer journeys and probably his final one to Rome where Mark may have written his gospel. The doctrinal attitudes displayed in the book go a long way towards reconciling the attitudes of Peter and Paul, though it is impossible to say whether these were present in the original or whether elements have been added by a later hand.

If the book was written in Italy as is generally supposed, it was aimed at the very large Jewish diaspora there, but it did not exclude the Gentile poor—freedman and slave, male and female—who craved relief from Caesarean oppression.

Mark is the shortest of the four books and in some ways the most revealing. It has probably been heavily bowdlerised and certainly additions have been made. For example, a final passage purporting to recount Jesus' resurrection is so patently a fraud that it has now been dropped from all standard editions of the Bible. But it retains two elements which are indispensable to an understanding of both the expectations of the early Christians and of the primitive superstitions with which their minds were filled.

In the first place, there is a much greater conviction in Mark that Jesus would return to establish the earthly Kingdom he promised within the lifetime of the writer than in the later books when hope began to fade and a heavenly Kingdom had to be invented to take its place.[10]

Secondly, the work is dominated by what seems to the modern reader a distasteful, even nauseous obsession with demons. To Mark and, more importantly, to his Jesus, the reality of these demons was unquestioned. At times they seem more populous than the human beings they supposedly torment and throughout his ministry Jesus seems to have spent an inordinate amount of time in conversation with them.

His first encounter with these mysterious creatures occurs at the beginning of his ministry just after he has enlisted the disciples. They go to a synagogue in Capernaum in Galilee where there is a man possessed of an 'unclean spirit'.

The spirit calls out to Jesus: 'What have you to do with us, Jesus of Nazareth? Have you come to destroy us? I know who you are, the Holy One of God.'

Jesus: 'Be silent and come out of him!' And, says Mark, 'The unclean spirit, convulsing him and crying with a loud Voice, came out of him'.

The people are astonished because, as they say, 'With authority he even commands the unclean spirits and they obey him'. It is this power over demons which, according to Mark, causes Jesus' fame to spread.

Interestingly, the demons are not only controlled by Jesus but are well acquainted with him. As Mark says, '…he would not permit the demons to speak because they knew him'.[11]

Jesus' next significant encounter with them is the well-known episode of the Gadarene (or Gerasene) swine. On a visit to the Gadarenes he is accosted by a man possessed of many demons. Jesus has a conversation with them.

Jesus: 'Come out of the man, you unclean spirit!'

Demon(s): 'What have you to do with me, Jesus, son of the Most High God? I adjure you, by God, do not torment me.'

Jesus: 'What is your name?'

Demon(s): 'My name is Legion; for we are many.' The Demon then begs Jesus not to send him (them) out of the country. It spies a herd of swine feeding nearby.

Demon: 'Send us to the swine. Let us enter them.'

Jesus agrees immediately and the demons enter the herd of pigs which stampedes into the sea and all are drowned, though it is unknown whether the demons themselves perished in the process.[12]

There are some which give him more than the usual concern. On one occasion a man in a congregation calls out: 'Teacher, I brought my son to you, for he has a dumb spirit; and whenever it seizes him it dashes him down; and he foams and grinds his teeth and becomes rigid; and I asked your disciples to cast it out and they were not able.'

Jesus is disgusted: 'O faithless generation, how long am I to be with you? How long am I to bear with you? Bring him to me.'

The father brings the boy but upon seeing Jesus, the spirit convulses the lad, who falls to the ground foaming at the mouth and rolling about.

Jesus: 'How long has he had this?'

The father: 'From childhood. And it has often cast him into the fire and into the water to destroy him; but if you can do anything have pity on us and help us.'

Jesus: 'If you can! All things are possible to him who believes.'

The father: 'I believe; help my unbelief!'

Jesus (to the demon): 'You dumb and deaf spirit, I command you, come out of him and never enter him again.'

After one last convulsion the demon does as it is ordered. A little ashamed that they had not been able to effect the exorcism, the disciples ask, 'Why could we not cast it out?'

Jesus: 'This kind cannot be driven out by anything but prayer.'[13]

Curiously, it is not recorded that Jesus prayed. Perhaps this is an indication of the distance Christian attitudes had travelled in the decades between his death and the writing of the gospel.

From the earthly Messiah, a genuine human being who believed himself to have been chosen by Yahweh to bring about the end of the Last Times and to usher in the Kingdom of God on earth, Jesus was now beginning to assume a God-like air himself and a communion with Yahweh which no longer necessitated prayer.

The reason for this concentration on the demonology of Mark—which assumes a less prominent place in Matthew and Luke and only passing reference in John—is to illustrate at the outset the state of mind and the level of sophistication of both the gospel writers and of Jesus himself.

The image of Jesus which now prevails derives from a constant promotional up-dating of the character portrayed in the gospels.[14] It is apparently based on the premise that he is alive and well and sitting on the right hand of Power and presumably informed of all the scientific and societal advances made since those dark demon-ridden days and nights of 2,000 years ago. Of all the gospels, Mark is the most effective in evoking the real state of the man's mind and the times in which he lived.

One other aspect of Mark which throws light on the origin is its form. More than a third of it is devoted to the final week of Jesus' life in Jerusalem. There is no Sermon on the Mount as in Matthew or Luke (where it is the Sermon on the Plain) and very little attempt to place his activities prior to the Passover week in a cogent sequence. Indeed, some scholars have seen it as 'the passion with a preface'.[15] So in the unlikely events that Mark did gather some of his material from the reflections of Peter they were concentrated, it seems, not in a celebration of his life but the manner of his death.

MATTHEW

Opinion is divided on the place of origin of the Gospel According to Matthew, with rival claims for Syria and Alexandria in Egypt. During the war with Rome many thousands of Jewish refugees fled both north and south, members of the apostolic community among them, and in each case the early Christians would have approved Matthew's work which combined both Western and Eastern elements in the narrative.

Part of the confusion arises from the mistaken belief over many centuries that Matthew was the first of the four gospels to be composed (hence its placement in the New Testament). The basis of this belief was a statement from Papias that 'Matthew compiled the Oracles in the Hebrew language, and each interpreted them as he was able'. However, it is now universally accepted that the gospel was composed in Greek and that its author was almost certainly non-Jewish. The oracles referred to were probably the Old Testament prophesies which may have been compiled in the Logia and used as a basis for the much larger work.[16] The internal evidence suggests that the book was written in Alexandria and designed to appeal to the very large Jewish community there as well as the new Christian converts.

Only in Matthew, for example, does the infant Jesus escape to Egypt with his mother and father to avoid the murderous Herod who, according to the gospel, ordered the killing of 'all the male children in Bethlehem and in all that region who were two years old or under'.[17]

There is no supporting evidence whatever, either in biblical or secular records, for this Herodian atrocity and it is clearly a fabrication. But it strongly parallels a most important Jewish-Egyptian tradition, that of the Passover, when in the time of Jewish bondage Yahweh himself 'passed over' Egypt and slew all Egyptian male children under the age of two in vengeance.

Matthew is the first to introduce the concept of the virgin birth and this would be well received in a land where the God-mother, Isis, accomplished this remarkable feat in producing her son, Horus, many centuries earlier.

There is also an early Christian tradition that Mark spent time in Egypt before the production of his gospel and that he actually appointed Alexandria's first Christian bishop, Annianus[18] in A.D. 61-62. If this is true the author of the second gospel would have been well aware of Mark's standing in the church and this would help to account for the almost complete incorporation of Mark in the Matthew gospel—more than 600 verses from a possible 661.

But the book's place of origin is less important than its distinctive characteristics, the most striking being its obsessive need to relate Jesus' activities from birth to death to the messianic prophecies of the Old Testament. It is this overriding need which causes Jesus to be born in Bethlehem, born of a virgin, to flee to Egypt, to be tempted by the devil in the wilderness, to retreat when John the Baptist is arrested, to cast out demons, to ride an ass (and simultaneously a colt!) into Jerusalem, to speak in parables and so on. Even when Matthew quotes directly from Mark the author apparently feels an obligation to relate the activity to some prophetic reference from either the Old Testament or one of the non-canonised messianic books circulating at the time.

The effect is to damage the gospel's credibility. The reader cannot escape the view that the author would not be beyond rearranging his 'facts' to suit the demands of prophecy and in a number of cases, as will be illustrated, this is precisely what has happened.

The form of the book also indicates that the author had access to the 'Q' document which, it is supposed, told of Jesus' sayings and parables. Since that document is lost (if it ever really existed) it is not possible to say what liberties he took with it. But from these three sources—Mark and the two documents—and with imaginative additions from his own environment, the author has produced a work which for many

Christians is the standard biography of Jesus, 'the greatest story ever told'.[19]

The gospel is not, in fact, a biography as we understand the term today. Rather it is an uneasy combination of the author's own convictions about Jesus based upon fragmentary and uncertain reportage and his own fanatical need to persuade others of the rightness of his case. The resulting picture is of a curiously distorted figure at the heart of the narrative. Seen as literature (as so many Christians seem to feel obliged to view it) the work is not impressive.

LUKE

Luke is the 'romantic' version of the New Testament story. The Jesus portrayed there is a much gentler soul than the irascible mystic of Mark or the hellfire and damnation thunderer of Matthew.

In Luke, Jesus' actions seem to spring from an innate virtuousness, a compulsion as the Son of God to teach and to heal the rather pathetic human figures which surround him. His miracles are more elaborate, his parables more kindly, his manner more detached from the sweaty crowds which followed him and pressed upon him.

One reason for this is that by the time Luke was written—perhaps A.D. 105—Christians had gained a well-deserved reputation as haters of humanity, an intense inward-looking sect contemptuous of the world around them.[20] Luke was in part an attempt to counter this view among the Greek-speaking community where the book was written.

An equally notable characteristic is the author's attempt to round out the story into a coherent biography. To accomplish this he borrowed quite unashamedly from both biblical and secular sources. As well as Mark and other primitive documents circulating at the time, the author commandeered sections of the Old Testament and the writings of Josephus. This will be dealt with in greater detail in the various phases of Jesus' life but even the most superficial reading of the gospel reveals a series of parallels which is, to say the least, suspicious.

For example, the famed Magnificat, a poem in Luke attributed to Jesus' mother, Mary, is simply a re-working of the prayer of Hannah which is found in 1 Samuel 2.[21] In fact, Luke draws very heavily on 1 Samuel in the account of Jesus' birth and boyhood and at one stage appropriates verbatim a verse to keep his narrative flowing: 'Now the boy Samuel (Jesus) continued to grow both in stature and in favour with the Lord and with men'.[22]

The author is similarly indebted to Josephus, particularly for the census which, according to Luke, caused the family to journey from Nazareth to Bethlehem (where supposedly Joseph was born) for Jesus' own birth in the celebrated manger. This device allows him to date the birth, declare a prophecy fulfilled and avoid a judgement relished by the Jews at the time that 'nothing good can come out of Nazareth'.[23]

Another suspicious example comes from the autobiography of Josephus. When referring to his boyhood, the historian writes: 'While still a mere boy, about fourteen years old, I won universal applause for my love of letters; insomuch that the chief priests and learned men of the city (Jerusalem) used constantly to come to me for precise information on some particular of our ordinances'.

This was just the kind of useful, if immodest, anecdote which the author of Luke could borrow and adapt to a twelve-year-old Jesus in the Temple to help fill the empty years between his birth and the beginning of his ministry. But the incident as it appears in Luke has a larger significance than simply 'rounding out' his central character. It also has theological overtones and these sit well with his desire to present a character acceptable to both messianic Jews and to his Gentile readership. By having Jesus speak of the Temple as 'my Father's house' he implies that Jesus was aware of his divinity even in childhood, an attitude highly acceptable to the Greeks and just ambiguous enough to avoid alienating the messianic Jews.

Thus and throughout, Luke attempts to have the best of both worlds—a Jesus who is both an earthly, human Messiah and the divine son of God.

Unquestionably, there is a good deal in Luke to be gleaned in building an accurate picture of Jesus the man and the forces which drove him. But the clues must be selected with great care. As a whole, the work is self-serving and inaccurate; so much so that, unlike Matthew which is simply incompetent, the activist biographer of Luke could almost be said to have perpetrated a deliberate fraud. Its one saving grace is that it is such an easily detectable fraud. That kind of naivety has a certain ingenuous appeal.

JOHN

The fourth gospel has been a terrible embarrassment to Christians and a source of endless confusion to biblical scholars from the very beginning. In general, Mark, Matthew and Luke parallel each other in the settings and the staging of the various physical incidents which occurred in Jesus' life. They could hardly do otherwise since the later books were copied in great measure from the earlier ones, but Christian apologists have chosen to see this coincidence of events and sayings as somehow adding to their authenticity. They have coined the term synoptic meaning 'viewed together' which tends to imply that three separate viewpoints all agreed on the basic elements of Jesus' life and teaching. However, the main value of the term lies in differentiating them from the fourth gospel which contradicts them time and again, not only in detail but in central theological issues.

John is more than likely the last of the four to be written and its author, who lived in Asia Minor, was probably one John the Elder, bishop of Ephesus. It would have been composed after A.D. 115.

Over the centuries the gospel has often been ascribed to John the disciple who is usually linked with his brother, James, as the sons of Zebedee and to whom Jesus gave the name Boanerges (Thunderers). This is now regarded by scholars as absurd. The fisherman son of Zebedee the Galilean could no more have written it than Pontius Pilate himself. The Gnostic message it preaches is totally foreign to the Jewish disciples and indeed to Jesus who would have been bemused by it.

Part of the reason for the error is the presence in the story of the so-called Beloved Disciple whom it was thought could refer to John the disciple. But this, too, is false. The Beloved Disciple almost certainly owned a house in Jerusalem and John the fisherman did not. Jesus' relationship with the Beloved Disciple was quite different from his attitude to John who was certainly in his inner circle but was treated with no more affection than Andrew, Peter or the rest. The Beloved Disciple, like the gospel itself, is a special case.

He is another source of confusion in deciding the authorship of the book for it is clear that, unlike the synoptic gospels, there are two different hands at work in its composition. This has led most modern scholars to the conclusion that while it was written by John the Greek Elder (who also composed the Epistle standing in his name and the Book of Revelation) he worked from the reminiscences of the Beloved Disciple.

There is no way of knowing whether these were transmitted orally or were recorded in some document now lost. The passage of time from the events described—some eighty years— counts strongly against the likelihood of a personal relationship between the author and the disciple but does not rule it out completely. Early Christian tradition has it that John the Elder lived to a very advanced age and the gospel itself reports the widespread belief that the Beloved Disciple would not die until Jesus came again.[24]

But whatever the relationship (if any) between the disciple and the Elder, the internal evidence of the Gospel only alienates the author from his principal source. The disciple was a Jew, yet John contains some of the most sickening anti-Semitic diatribes in the whole of the New Testament (and as such must bear at least part of the responsibility for the most repugnant acts in human history). The disciple knew Jesus to believe himself to be the Messiah, yet in the hands of the Greek Elder this Jewish concept has disappeared almost completely. Jesus is a deity—the Son of God and very nearly His co-equal, the Gnostic leader of the forces of light against those of darkness. The prospect of an imminent Kingdom of Heaven on earth has passed and the author addresses the theological and metaphysical problems the faded hope left in its wake. And, to cap the argument, the author specifically dissociates himself from his source in two 'footnotes' within the narrative—John 19:35 and 21:24.

But the testimony of the Beloved Disciple and the part he played in Jesus' life are two vital clues in lifting the mask which the organised Church has placed over the real persona of Jesus and will be dealt with in greater detail in the narrative.

THE GOSPELS

No four books have ever been as minutely dissected as the gospels. Unfortunately, the most devoted of the vivisectors have invariably been convinced Christians seeking further sustenance for their faith. Invariably, they have found it, but not because of the rational persuasiveness nor even because of the forcefulness of the literary imagery to be found there. As advocacies they are singularly unconvincing and as literature they owe a great deal to the refinement of the court of King James. It is the certainty of their authors' convictions concerning the central character of the drama which has given the seekers the will to continue to reject the tapping hammer of reason. Indeed, it has often been suggested that this very quality, this sense of utter conviction among the gospel writers, is further proof—if it were needed—of the truth of their message.

This argument would certainly have weight if the gospels were unique in this respect, but of course they are not. Utter conviction is the abiding characteristic of all religious writing from the Koran to the sayings of Confucius to the revelations of Joseph Smith in his 'Book of Mormon'. It is true of Karl Marx and Mao ZeDong. It is true of the Flat Earthers and the Rosicrucians and the Masons and the Fascisti. It is true, too, of nihilists and those atheists who have turned their unbelief into a mirror image of the very thing they most detest. It is also true of those who say there was no Jesus, that he was simply the product of a strange delusion. Jesus lived. Jesus died. The gospels hold many of the clues to enable the modern reader to fill the void between those two historic events, to come to grips with the secret life, hidden by the obfuscation of the faithful over twenty centuries of changing times.

Notes

1. Authorities disagree on the precise dating. The more 'orthodox' the authority, the earlier the dating. The figures used here rely most heavily on the work of Schonfield and the Encyclopaedia Britannica.

2. Author of History of the Jewish War (C. A.D. 78), The Antiquities of the Jews (C. A.D. 95), and his autobiography, Against Apion (C. A.D. 100).

3. Antiquities of the Jews.

4. A Roman historian, who wrote in A.D. 115 of the reign of Nero and the burning of Rome in A.D. 64. At that time, he said, there was 'a race of men detested for their evil practices, and commonly called Chrestiani. The name was derived from Chrestus who, in the reign of Tiberius, suffered under Pontius Pilate, Procurator of Judea. By that event the sect of which he was the founder received a blow which for some time checked the growth of a dangerous superstition; but it revived soon after and spread with recruited vigour not only in Judea...but even in the city of Rome, the common sink into which everything infamous and abominable flows like a torrent from all quarters of the World. 'He goes on to claim that Nero used the Chrestiani as a scapegoat for the disaster.

5. The Governor of Bithynia wrote to the Emperor Trajan in A.D. 110 for advice on how to handle the new sect: 'This contagious superstition is not confined to the cities, but has spread through the villages and the countryside'. It is the first mention of the sect in pagan literature.

6. Had the 'miracles' of Jesus been known to Paul—and if they occurred they surely would have been—it is inconceivable that he would not have at least mentioned them.

7. Peter 5:13.

8. Acts 11:2-3.

9. Probably a bishop of Hierapolis in western Asia Minor. Interestingly, he is regarded by Eusebius of Caesarea (4th century) from whom most of his work has come down to us as 'unintelligent' (from Eusebius, Church History).

10. Mark 13:30.

11. Mark 1:23-26, 34.

12. Mark 5:1-13.

13. Mark 9:18-29.

14. Jesus Christ Superstar; Godspell.

15. Bauer.

16. In the form of a papyrus or leather scroll.

17. Matthew 2:16.

18. Hebrew: Hananiah.

19. Daryl F. Zanuck.

20. This was a natural consequence of their belief that the end of the world was imminent and that the essentially sinful nature of man would be forever condemned to hellfire and damnation.

21. Luke 1:46-55; 1 Samuel 2:1-10.

22. 1 Samuel 2:26.

23. John 1:46—'Can anything good come out of Nazareth?'

24. John 21:23.

PART 2

The Evidence

5

Birth and Childhood

THE first and fourth gospels (Mark and John) ignore Jesus' birth: Mark, because if the author knew the circumstances they were not regarded as either fitting or significant enough to warrant mention; John, because by then Jesus was not really human—his presence in the physical world had been a visitation from God and the earthiness of childbirth had no place in the author's vision.

So it was left to the two great elaborators, Matthew and Luke, to place their distinctive stamps on the occasion and they did so in a manner which illustrates their abiding characteristics very aptly.

According to Matthew, Mary is betrothed to Joseph but before they marry it is discovered that she is with child. Her fiancé resolves to 'divorce'[1] her quietly but before he has the chance to do so an angel appears to him in a dream saying, 'Do not fear to take Mary (as) your wife for that which is conceived in her is of the Holy Spirit'.[2] Joseph complies and also forbears to have sexual relations with her until after the birth.

Matthew tells the story of the three wise men from the East who follow a star to Bethlehem and who meet Herod the Great on the way. On hearing that the travellers are on the track of the birth of a new king of the Jews, Herod asks them to call back after they have found him to report his whereabouts.

The wise men duly find the family in a house in Bethlehem (there is no mention of a manger in a stable) and shortly after the birth present him with their gold, frankincense and myrrh. Having been warned in a dream not to report back to Herod they return quickly to their own country.

According to Matthew, the reason the child is born in Bethlehem is simply to fulfil the prophecy in the Old Testament (Micah 2:5):

> And you, O Bethlehem, in the land of Judah, are by no means least among the rulers of Judah; for from you shall come a ruler who will govern my people Israel.

Luke is much more detailed in his treatment of both the conception and the birth of Jesus. His story begins not with Jesus but with the begetting of John the Baptist whom, he indicates, is related to Jesus on his mother's side.

A priest name Zachariah, a man of advanced years, is married to a woman of similar age called Elizabeth; they have no children. The angel Gabriel appears to Zachariah and tells him that he and Elizabeth will have a son whom they should call John. Gabriel also tells him that until the birth he will be struck dumb. According to Luke this is exactly what happens.

Elizabeth duly conceives (though it is unclear whether Zachariah or Gabriel is the cause) and because of her age 'hides herself' for the next five months.

In the sixth month of Elizabeth's pregnancy Gabriel is again called to duty and appears to a virgin, Mary of Nazareth, in the province of Galilee. As with Matthew, Mary is betrothed to Joseph but not yet married. Gabriel tells her that because she has found favour with God she will conceive and bear a son to be called Jesus. Mary is startled by the news—'I have no husband'—but Gabriel reassures her and tells her of the similar experience of her kinswoman Elizabeth. Mary falls in with the idea and on this occasion it is clear that the Holy Spirit is the cause of the conception, though it takes place some time afterwards.

Mary resolves to visit Elizabeth in a city in the hills of the province of Judea and when she arrives both the woman and the unborn child are delighted to see her: 'The babe in my womb leapt for joy'.[3] Mary stays with her kinswoman during the last three months of her confinement but leaves before the actual birth of John. By then, we are told, she herself has become pregnant.

No mention is made of Joseph's reaction to his betrothed's condition and Luke introduces the story of a census ordered by Caesar Augustus which requires Joseph to register himself at his birthplace, Bethlehem. Drawing from Josephus, Luke says the census was that carried out when Quirinius was Legate of Syria. The discovery of this fact in a secular source was fortuitous indeed. But, as will be seen, it created the problem of co-ordinating the timetable of Jesus' life with the other, earlier account.

In his narrative, Luke then tells the story of Jesus' birth in the manger and while there is no mention of the wise men the birth is attended by shepherds alerted to the event by a multitude of angels. The shepherds tell Joseph and Mary about the angelic visitation but, according to Luke, Mary is unresponsive: 'Mary kept all these things, pondering them in her heart'.[4]

The child is not immediately named. The parents wait for eight days and after he is circumcised call him Jesus and journey to nearby Jerusalem where they sacrifice either 'a pair of turtle doves or two young pigeons'.[5]

While in the Temple they are approached by an old priest named Simeon and an ancient prophetess, Anna, both of whom predict great things for the infant. Nowhere else are Simeon and Anna mentioned but it is significant that in the Old Testament story of Samuel, from which Luke drew other details, the child's mother is herself named Anna.

In addition to Matthew and Luke there are two other sources which separately record the birth of Jesus: the Talmud, the written collection of Jewish Law, tradition and custom regarded by Jews as second in importance only to the Old Testament; and the Koran, the sacred book of the Moslems written in about A.D. 600, which preserves oral traditions from a much earlier time.

The version in the Koran deserves to be quoted in full:

> And you shall recount in the book the story of Mary: how she left her people and betook herself to a solitary place to the east.
>
> We sent to her our spirit in the semblance of a full grown man. And when she saw him she said: 'May the merciful defend me from you! If you fear the Lord, leave me and go your way.'
>
> 'I am the messenger of your Lord,' he replied, 'and I have come to give you a holy son.'
>
> 'How shall I bear a son,' she answered, 'when I am a virgin untouched by man?'
>
> 'Such is the will of your Lord,' he replied, 'that is no difficult thing for Him. "He shall be a sign to Mankind," says the Lord, "and a blessing from Ourself. This is our decree."'
>
> Thereupon she conceived him, and retired to a far-off place. And when she felt the throes of childbirth she lay down by the trunk of a palm tree crying, 'Oh would that I had died and passed into oblivion!'
>
> But a voice from below cried out to her: 'Do not despair. Your Lord has provided a brook that runs at

your feet, and if you shake the trunk of this palm tree it will drop fresh ripe dates into your lap. Therefore rejoice. Eat and drink and should you meet any mortal say to him: "I have vowed a fast to the Merciful and will not speak with any man today."'

Then she took the child to her people, who said to her: 'This is indeed a strange thing! Sister of Aaron, your father was never a whoremonger, nor was your mother a harlot.'

She made a sign to them, pointing to the child. But they replied 'How can we speak with a babe in the cradle?' Whereupon he spoke and said: 'I am the servant of Allah. He has given me the gospel and ordained me a prophet. His blessing is upon me wherever I go, and he has commanded me to be steadfast in prayer and to give alms to the poor as long as I shall live. He has exhorted me to honour my mother and has purged me of vanity and wickedness. I was blessed on the day I was born and blessed shall I be on the day of my death; and my peace be upon me on the day when I shall be raised to life.'

Such was Jesus, the son of Mary. That is the whole truth which they are unwilling to accept. Allah forbids that He himself should beget a son! When He decrees a thing He need only say "Be" and it is.

Allah is my Lord and your Lord. Therefore serve Him. That is the right path.

Yet the sects are divided concerning Jesus. But when the fateful day arrives woe to the unbelievers! Their sight and hearing shall be sharpened on the day when they appear before us. Truly the unbelievers are in the grossest error.

The Talmudic writers of the first and second centuries took a much more down-to-earth view of the event. According to them, Jesus was born an illegitimate son of a Roman soldier called Panther (Panthera). He worked magic, ridiculed the wise, seduced and stirred up the people, gathered five disciples[6] about him and was hanged (crucified) on the eve of a Passover.

It is clear that the four versions of the conception and birth now extant share only one common denominator. All are agreed that the conception took place before Jesus' mother was married.

The two gospel versions insist that Mary was engaged to be married at the time and Matthew records the understandable pique of the prospective bridegroom when he discovers his bride-to-be's condition.[7] Luke and the Koran have Mary taking a journey away from Nazareth during which the child is conceived. The gospels and the Muslim holy book ascribe the conception to the Holy Spirit either in the form of the angel Gabriel (despite the fact that Jesus himself says angels are asexual), or the semblance of a full-grown man. The less romantic Talmud even names the Roman soldier involved.

If the Talmudic version is to be credited it must be understood that such incidents were commonplace in Palestine at the time. Armies of occupation are notorious for their treatment of the women of the subject nation and the Romans in troublesome Galilee were no exception. They took their pleasure where they could find it and a girl travelling alone would be easy prey.

But to a Jewish girl from the Galilean 'bible belt', the experience would be the ultimate defilement. It would be unthinkable for her to admit to her parents that such a thing had occurred and she would go to any lengths to provide an alternative explanation for her pregnancy. To confess to rape was to be branded unclean, a harlot, by her own straight-laced community.

All this would be of only marginal interest if it were the only evidence upon which to base a judgement on what actually happened. Myths and legend surrounding the birth of a significant figure abound in all religious writing.

The Persian word saviour (saoshyant) arises from an expression denoting Zarathustra's seed in a virgin. Buddha is associated with a virginal conception, emerging from Maya's right side ten months after his mother's left side had been pierced by a mysterious white elephant. The birth of Mohammed is promised to his mother by an angel. The birth of Confucius was attended by angels.

It is true that, unlike the others, Jesus' conception is surrounded by what a modern court of law would term 'suspicious circumstances' and from one source at least a quite specific allegation. Certainly, it would be difficult today to answer the charge with a resort to divine intervention (though it is not unknown).

It would also not be unusual in the circumstances for the newly married couple, aware of the woman's condition, to go on a long journey and return only after the birth of the child.

But even this would not be worth serious consideration without supportive evidence from Jesus' later life—his activities as a youth and man, his attitudes to authority, his sayings and perhaps even the manner of his death. Whether that evidence exists in fact will be seen as we proceed.

Meanwhile, there are two elements of the gospel versions of the birth which have an important bearing on the consideration of Jesus' life as a whole. The first is his name.

NAME

The child was not named Jesus but Yesu'a (or Yeshu'a), the equivalent of Joshua in modern English. The Greeks rendered this as Iesous and in turn the Romans translated it as Iesus before it found the English pronunciation Jesus and returned to the New Testament in that form. The significance, however, is not one of pronunciation. Far more important to the child and the man who bore it was the meaning of the name: 'The Help of Yahweh' (also 'Yahweh saves').

Undoubtedly, a person's name can have a considerable effect upon his self-image, not only as he repeats it to himself but as others react to him through the name. This is probably much less true today than in former times when names took the form of descriptive labels. But even now the concept has considerable force.[8]

To a Jewish boy in Galilee at a time of the most intense religious fervour— particularly if his parentage was in any way questionable—the phrase by which he was known could be expected to have a very considerable effect. It is not at all difficult to imagine such a child forced to spend long hours at a trade for which he was temperamentally unsuited, developing the vision of himself as 'The Help of Yahweh' bound to the workshop when he might be out in the world accomplishing great things. As he showed in later life when he changed the name of his disciple Simon to Peter (Greek: Cephas, the Rock) and that of the sons of Zebedee to The Thunderers, Jesus himself was very conscious of the importance of names.[9] This consciousness could hardly have arisen without his being affected by it himself.

DATE

Also significant in the birth stories is the dating of the event implied in each. According to Matthew the birth took place during the reign of Herod the Great. However, it is known that Herod died in 4 B.C. Luke says he was born during the census called by Quirinius, the Legate of Syria. However, it is known that this took place in the year A.D. 6-7, thus we find a discrepancy of at least ten years.

The possibility that Jesus was actually born at the end of A.D. 1 is rarely considered and with good reason. The man who calculated this date and in doing so invented the Christian Era was one Dionysius Exiguus, a monk in Italy who in A.D. 525 made the necessary calculations at the request of Pope Saint John 1. He decided that Jesus was born 753 years after the date of the founding of the city of Rome.

The good monk was aware that according to Matthew—then regarded as the authoritative gospel because of the mistaken belief that it was the first written—the birth occurred during the reign of Herod the Great. But unhappily, in one of the more piquant accidents of history, the poor fellow made a mistake. He was out by at least three years. Herod was well and truly dead 750 years (not 753) after the founding of Rome, but the miscalculation was not discovered for another 200 years. In the 8th century an Englishman, the Venerable Bede, questioned the chronology and in the 9th century the German monk, Regino of Prum, rejected it utterly. But by then the Era was enshrined so the matter was quietly put aside.

Those who prefer the Lucan version point to the assertion in Luke that Jesus began his ministry in the fifteenth year of the reign of Tiberius when he was 'about thirty'.[10] Clearly, Luke has made the calculation himself so it is consistent with the later birthdate. But because there is such a paucity of hard evidence in the gospels, anything which appears to confirm an alleged fact is quickly seized upon.

The only other reference to his age is found in John where, during his ministry, he is said to be 'not yet fifty'[11], a very large difference for a time when life expectancy rarely exceeded sixty years. But it is understandable that some religious image-makers should have preferred the Lucan calculation. It is much more difficult for potential converts to conceive of a Son of God bordering on middle age, and of course the younger the man, the more attractive a figure he presents, the more wonderful appear the insights expressed in his sayings.

One final element which sheds light on the authors' attitudes—if not the birth itself—is the compilation of genealogies designed to show Jesus' illustrious lineage. Over the centuries these have caused much argument in Christian circles since they differ so widely. If one is true the other is false.

Matthew traces Jesus' ancestry back forty generations to Abraham while Luke goes even further, a full seventy-six generations to Adam and God himself. Both are obvious fabrications and the Paul condemns such activity as worthless sophistry. The authors, however, recognised their value to messianic Jews, for in each case they established Jesus as a direct descendant of David and according to many prophecies it was from the House of David that the Messiah would arise.

But in both gospels there is a strange contradiction. The parental line is traced not from Mary but from Joseph, despite the fact that both writers insist that Joseph was not the father. In this they reveal that the concept of Davidic descent preceded the belief in the virgin birth—small wonder that a study of the genealogies does not occupy a prominent place in modern Christian teaching.

The first and fourth gospels pass over Jesus' childhood without mention and it falls to Matthew and Luke to fill the gap. Unfortunately, in neither case do they make a serious effort to do so.

As has been mentioned, Matthew (and only Matthew) tells the story of the flight to Egypt to escape the Herodian sword.

There is no other evidence whatever, whether biblical or secular, to support the claim, and Matthew further damages his case by asserting that the journey 'fulfilled prophecy'.

According to the story the family stayed in Egypt until the death of Herod when an angel appeared to Joseph advising him to return. But since Herod's son, Archelaus, reigned over Judea in his place, Joseph decided, on the basis of a dream, to pass through the south and settle in Nazareth, Galilee, the first mention in Matthew of the town where traditionally he spent his early years (despite the fact that there are no records of its existence until several centuries later).

Matthew says nothing of the period the family supposedly spent in Egypt though later apocryphal works are less reticent. In a gospel of Thomas, for example, Jesus and Mary stay with a widow but are asked to leave after Jesus brings a dried fish to life and then turns it into water. In other similar works, mother and son are accompanied by one Salome who has acted as midwife and who stays with Jesus throughout his life. As a child, Jesus is often pictured at play doing small miracles: modelling twelve sparrows from clay then bringing them to life; killing his playmates in a fit of pique and returning them to life as his anger cools. There are simple stories of him as an eight-year-old helping his father in his carpentry workshop, miraculously lengthening a piece of timber which had been too short for the job, or healing the foot of a careless woodcutter.

However, none of these stories are taken seriously by modern scholars and Matthew is quite silent about the vital years of Jesus' development until he is baptised by John and comes to public attention as an adult.

Luke is only slightly more forthcoming with his single story of the family at a Passover celebration in Jerusalem. When the ritual feasting and sacrificing are done, the family sets out with their group to return to Nazareth and after a day's march realise Jesus is not with them. They return to the city and eventually find him in the Temple talking with the priests who are obviously impressed by his intelligence.

When his mother questions him he replies that he must be in his 'Father's house'.[12] Neither parent understands his meaning (though if Luke's conception story is to be believed, Mary's ignorance is hard to comprehend) and they set off again for Nazareth.

As in Matthew, Luke is silent about the formative years of Jesus' life and this paucity of information has brought about an undue concentration on the incident in the Temple. If it did occur—and this is doubtful, given Luke's willingness to borrow from Josephus— it reveals a Jesus already preoccupied with his Father, a continuing and haunting image throughout the records of his public ministry.

Unlike the stories of his birth, there are no alternative sources from which to glean an understanding of these missing years. But in the four gospels themselves there are a number of indications, both in his words and actions, of the way in which this vital period was spent. One of the most significant areas is his relationship with his family.

Notes

1. Matthew 1:19.
2. Matthew 1:20-21.
3. Luke 1:44.
4. Luke 2:19.
5. Luke 2:24.
6. Matthai, Naki, Nitser, Buni and Todah.
7. Matthew 1:20.
8. As Hollywood agents—and the Cyrils of the world—would readily attest.
9. Also Levi to Matthew—'the Gift of Yahweh'.
10. Luke 3:23.
11. John 8:57.
12. Luke 2:49.

6

The Family

A CLEAR knowledge of Jesus' relationship with his family is central to an understanding of the man and his mission. Yet it is an area which has received scant attention from orthodox scholars. Indeed, so little has it been explored the layman would assume that references to it in the gospels were few and inconclusive. As will be seen, this is not true.

The neglect stems in part from the Church's desire to present Jesus as a deity. He must be kept separate from the earthly joys and the inevitable tragedies, the bickering and the pain of a large, opinionated family. He must be seen as a lone, tortured figure beyond all human bondage. In the Church's presentation, his only real connection with his family is through the love he allegedly bears for his mother. This, too, is inaccurate and there is an additional reason for the Church to discourage an examination of it.

During the Middle Ages a cult arose which was devoted to the Virgin Mother. It fulfilled a need within the religion, one which went back to the very earliest religious needs of mankind.[1] Recognising this, the Church did nothing to discourage it. By the 5th century hymns had been written in praise of her, by the 6th her name was introduced into the canon of the Mass and by the 10th it was widely believed that prayers addressed to her achieved miraculous results. Protestant churches have largely passed it by.

Before closely examining the relationship it would be useful to identify the family members as perceived by the gospel writers.

Mark carries no mention of Joseph the father. This is taken by some scholars to indicate that by the time Jesus' public ministry began—the point at which Mark starts his narrative—Joseph was no longer alive. Support can be adduced for this view. None of the gospels record his death during Jesus' ministry and none suggest that he took any part in it. None have him present at the crucifixion. In all four stories he simply passes out of the narrative prior to the time Jesus begins his preaching tours. It is negative evidence certainly, but in view of other indications involving Jesus' actions and teachings, it seems an acceptable option.

Mark does specifically mention Mary, Jesus' mother, and his brothers James, Joses, Judas and Simon. He also reports that Jesus had sisters, though he neither names them nor indicates how many.

Matthew says that in addition to Joseph and Mary the family included brothers James, Joseph (Joses in Mark), Simon and Judas, as well as sisters. The passage is almost certainly copied from Mark.

Luke is much less forthcoming on the question of siblings. The only indication of any earthly kin (other than Joseph and Mary and, through Mary, John the Baptist) is a reference during the crucifixion but even that is an oblique one. Present there, he says, was Mary, the mother of James the disciple. This is much more likely to refer to James Boanerges, son of Zebedee, than Jesus' brother, James.[2] But without it there is no reference whatever to either brothers or sisters. By the time Luke was written the process of deification was clearly well advanced.

John acknowledges Joseph and Mary to be his legal parents and mentions his brothers several times though they are not named. There is no indication of any sisters.

Nowhere is it suggested that Jesus was not the first-born of the family (on the contrary) and there is little reason to doubt it. However, if, as seems likely, his father died some time during his teens or young manhood Jesus would have naturally become head of the household, responsible not only for the day-to-day support of the family but the accumulation of respectable dowries for his sisters. To a humble carpenter this was certainly a full-time job and in such circumstances his decision to abandon the family for the life of an itinerant teacher assumes added significance. Obviously, he must have felt utterly compelled to take up his mission. Equally obviously, the decision must have caused great consternation within the family circle, perhaps to the point of a cleavage among its members. There are indications in Jesus' own words that just such a falling-out occurred. *Every single reference in every one of the gospels paints him as being positively hostile towards his family, and at times they towards him.*

In Mark, Jesus passes through the family seat in Galilee with his disciples and a considerable crowd. One day he is in a house surrounded by the faithful when the message is brought that his mother and brothers are outside asking for him.

He spurns them. 'Who are my mother and my brothers?' He looks around the room at the faithful and answers his own question. 'Here are my mother and brothers! Whoever does the will of God is my brother and sister, and mother.'[3]

On another occasion he returns to the Nazareth area and begins teaching in the synagogue but is met with blank stares. 'Is not this the carpenter, the son of Mary and brother of James and Joses and Judas and Simon, and are not his sisters here with us?' And, says Mark, 'they took offence'.

The feeling is reciprocated. Jesus replies: 'A prophet is not without honour, except in his own country...' then more specifically, '*and among his own kin, and in his own house.*'[4] [Italics mine]

The only other reference in the first gospel occurs at the crucifixion when his mother might have been present. She is not referred to as the mother of Jesus but as 'Mary, the mother of James the younger and Joses'—the names of two of Jesus' brothers.[5] But if it was Jesus' mother, no word passes between them.

In Matthew the incidents recorded in Mark are repeated with minor variations though the sense of antipathy within the family is unchanged. But as well as specific instances of family conflict, Matthew contains examples of Jesus' general attitude toward family relationships, an attitude which patently came from his own experience. Speaking of his mission, he says:

> 'For I have come to set a man against his father and a daughter against her mother and a daughter-in-law against her mother-in-law; and a man's foes will be those of his own household. He who loves father or mother more than me is not worthy of me...'[6]

Denouncing the accepted order of the Church, Jesus says: 'And call no man your father on earth, for you have one father, who is in heaven.'

As has been noted, Luke has excised from his work nearly all family references contained in the earlier gospels. Thus there is no mention of the rejection by Jesus of his mother and brothers and Luke's version of the incident in the synagogue near Nazareth when Jesus' teachings are spurned by the people is changed in a typically Lucan manner.

At first the people are listening approvingly, but then someone says, 'Is not this Joseph's son?'

Jesus' reaction is violent. 'Doubtless you will quote me this proverb, "Physician, heal yourself; what we have heard you did at Capernaum, do here in your own country."' (Jesus is reported in Luke to have cast out an 'unclean demon' from a man in Capernaum but strangely the incident occurs after his preaching in the Nazareth synagogue). He then goes on, 'No prophet is acceptable in his own country,' with all reference to the family deleted.[7]

The only other reference in Luke is to Mary and again Jesus seems to feel obliged to disparage her at every opportunity. While he is preaching a woman is overwhelmed by his words and cries out, 'Blessed is the womb that bore you and the breasts that you sucked.'

Jesus will have none of it. He replies, 'Blessed rather are those who hear the word of God and keep it.'[8]

In the small essay which forms the first section of the opening chapter of John, the author, speaking of Jesus, states quite plainly, 'He came to his own home and his own people received him not.' The general tenor of this remark is maintained throughout the gospel in all references to Jesus and his family.

John (and only John) relates the story of the first 'miracle'; that of turning water into wine at a wedding feast. The incident occurs at the instigation of his mother and it is a curious story. When the wine runs out during the celebrations Mary turns to Jesus and says, 'They have no wine.'

Jesus snaps a reply. 'O woman, what have you to do with me? My hour has not yet come.'

But instead of accepting the rebuff, Mary continues as though the words were never uttered. She turns to the servants and says, 'Do whatever he tells you.'[9]

Jesus then performs the miracle and afterwards, says John, his mother and brothers accompany him to Capernaum with his disciples.

On another occasion, having aroused the hatred of 'the Jews', Jesus decides not to go to Judea since they are seeking to kill him. At the time, says John, 'the Jews' feast of the Tabernacles was at hand [in Jerusalem]. So his brothers said to him, "Leave here and go to Judea, that your disciples may see the works you are doing. For no man works in secret if he seeks to be known openly. If you do these things, show yourself openly to the world." For even his brothers did not believe in him.'[10]

The passage clearly implies that Jesus' brothers sought to do him harm. It is nowhere suggested that the brothers were unaware of the desire of the Jews to kill him, and in the small, closed society of the time it would be absurd to suggest that they were ignorant of the threat, yet on the flimsiest grounds they suggest that he should expose himself to his enemies.

In the circumstances, Jesus' reply to his brothers is, to say the least, restrained: 'My time has not yet come,' he says. Then he reveals his own attitude towards them: 'But your time is always here. The world cannot hate you, but it hates me because I testify of it that its works are evil. Go to the feast yourselves; I am not going up to this feast for my time has not yet fully come.'[11]

John is much less ambiguous than the synoptics about the presence of Jesus' mother at the crucifixion. According to John, not only was she there but words passed between them. Seeing her standing near the Beloved Disciple, Jesus cries out from the cross: 'Woman, behold your son.' But the words probably refer not to himself but to the Beloved Disciple, for immediately afterwards he calls to that figure: 'Behold your mother,' and the disciple takes her to his own home. If this incident occurred, it probably says more about Jesus' relationship with the Beloved Disciple than with his mother.[12]

Notes

1. In this, Mary is the clear descendent of the God-mother, Isis of ancient Egypt who still retained a large following throughout the civilised world at the beginning of the Christian era.
2. See Matthew 20:20.
3. Mark 3:31-35.
4. Mark 6:2-6.
5. Mark 15:40
6. Matthew 10:35-37.
7. Luke 4:16-25.
8. Luke 11:27-28.
9. John 2:3-12.
10. John 7:1-5.
11. John 7:5-8.
12. The incident also lends weight to the view that Joseph, his legal father, had died.

7

The Human Figure

NONE of the canonised gospels or the Pauline epistles contain a direct description of Jesus' physical appearance. This might be simply because the authors had no knowledge of it, but, if that is the case it is curious that no such disability applied in the case of John the Baptist. One would have expected that if the Baptist's appearance were thought worthy of mention, particularly in Mark, the appearance of Jesus would be at least equally significant.

Of course this is only true if his appearance coincided with the image the writers and their copyists and translators were concerned to present. Put bluntly, if he were not a prepossessing individual the easiest solution to the dilemma would have been to delete a description altogether. There are indications that this is precisely what was attempted, for one or two remnants of description still persist.

The 1945 discovery of a Gospel of Thomas in Egypt[1] could well be significant. It contains a fairly detailed description of Jesus the man.

The authenticity of the Gospel of Thomas—in the sense that it faithfully reproduced the sayings and deeds of Jesus in line with the accepted gospel stories—is seriously questioned by the Church, as is the dating of the document which is thought to be second century A.D. But this does not invalidate the description of Jesus, and for very good reason. While the sayings it presents are intended to attract and sustain Christian adherents, the figure of Jesus it describes is not in itself attractive. He is said to be less than three cubits (168 centimetres) tall, with a very dark complexion, a bowed back, and a long face with bushy eyebrows which form a continuous line. If the author were simply creating a figure to inspire his readers to devotion he could hardly have chosen a less suitable image. Certainly, if he did faithfully reflect Jesus' appearance there is every reason to believe that such descriptions were quickly excised from the canonised gospels. It may well have been that because of its origin and use in Egypt, away from the mainstream of Christian development, the document escaped the censor's pen.

Also, if it is a true representation there are indications that the editors of the four canonised gospels did not delete all references and that echoes remain. For example, in Luke when Jesus is being rejected by the congregation in the Nazareth synagogue he replies: 'Doubtless you will quote to me this proverb, "Physician, heal yourself…"'[2] Such a statement makes no sense at all if the person who utters it is a strapping six-footer glowing with health, but it would certainly be appropriate to the figure described by Thomas.

There is also the necessity to engage Simon of Cyrene to carry Jesus' cross which is quite against the custom and would only be permitted if the condemned person were physically unable to bear it. It might be thought that Jesus was so seriously scourged by the soldiers that the beating weakened him but there is no strong indication of this.

There is Pilate's insistence in nailing to the top of the cross the written appellation, 'Jesus of Nazareth, King of the Jews'. His hatred of the Jews was intense and he clearly took considerable pleasure in the act.[3] This becomes much more comprehensible if Jesus was, physically at least, an insignificant figure, than if he were the perfect example of manhood so often portrayed in art.

Finally, there is the speed with which he died. Though there is a disparity between the synoptics and the fourth gospel—and limitless apologetic theories—it is universally accepted that he took less than a single day to die on the cross. This was an extraordinarily short period for a healthy individual in his prime. For example, Josephus quotes instances of men being brought down after two days on the cross and still surviving. Pilate himself was astonished at the speed with which he expired and took pains to confirm the death before agreeing that Jesus be taken down for burial.[4]

Unexpectedly, Thomas's description also provides further support for Jesus' unorthodox parentage. The name of his alleged father, Panther, sounds more like an agnomen or 'nickname' than the soldier's given name. And since the most striking attribute of the panther is its colour, it follows that he could well have had the dark complexion apparent in the description of the son.

It has been noted that a discrepancy exists in the gospels concerning Jesus' age at the beginning of his ministry. According to Luke he was 'about thirty' but according to John he was 'not yet fifty'. However, if it is accepted that he was born during the reign of Herod the Great (as Matthew asserts) some conclusions can be drawn.

It is known from Josephus that Pontius Pilate's term as Procurator of Judea began in A.D. 27 and ended in controversy in the latter part of A.D. 36. Therefore, the crucifixion of Jesus must have occurred—at the latest— during the Passover of A.D. 36. Because of Jesus' connection with John the Baptist, it follows that this was the fateful date.

The cause of the Baptist's imprisonment by Herod Antipas (Herod the Great's son) and his subsequent execution was, according to the gospels, John's denunciation of Herod's marriage to Herodias, the widow of his brother, Philip.[5] Since

Philip died late in A.D. 33 the marriage almost certainly took place in A.D. 34.

Herod's first wife, the daughter of Aretas, king of neighbouring Arabia Petraea, was outraged at her husband's faithlessness and returned to her father who immediately sought to avenge his daughter's honour and prepared for war against Herod.

Herod mobilised to defend himself and took the Baptist in chains to the fortified town of Machaerus near the Arabian border where he had established his headquarters. It was here that the Baptist was beheaded at the urging of Herod's new wife.

In the war which followed in A.D. 35 and 36 Herod was heavily defeated and according to Josephus many Jews regarded the defeat as divine judgement for the murder of John.

It follows that if Jesus was born during the reign of Herod the Great he could not have been less than thirty-eight years old when baptised by John just prior to his arrest. In that case, since his ministry probably lasted a little over two years, he would have been no less than forty years old when he died on the cross.

Notes

1. At Nag-Hammadi. A number of works were discovered on the site including (in addition to the Gospel) the Book of Thomas the Athlete, an 'infancy gospel' ascribed to Thomas and an Apocryphon (secret book) of James.
2. Luke 4:23.
3. John 19:19-22.
4. Mark 15:42-46.
5. Mark 6:17-19.

8

Miracles and Healings

IN the comparative enlightenment of the 20th century, secular scholars are much less willing to accept the historicity of the Sea Stories and Fish Stories[1] represented as miracles in the gospels. The parallels between these accounts and similar adventures of Old Testament prophets are simply too striking not to have been borrowed and burnished to enliven the Jesus legend. Indeed, it has been said that given the frequency of the accounts of Old Testament figures 'feeding the multitude'—and the all-too-obvious symbolism of the act—it would have been a miracle if such a story had not found its way into the gospels.[2]

There has also been a measure of hard-nosed logic applied to the claims of Jesus' control over the weather. If this were historically true, it is argued that there would have been no need for his fellow Jews to have faith in his kinship with Yahweh. The farmers of rural Palestine would have stampeded to reach his side. And if he really could raise people from the dead, half the nation would have flocked to him demanding the return of their loved ones. Such arguments have a simple clarity which cannot be denied.

In the more liberal theological circles, it has been appreciated that the destruction of much of Jerusalem, including the Temple in the great Jewish uprising of A.D. 66, allowed the gospel writers to ascribe to Jesus a 'prediction' of the event in the same way that many Old Testament 'prophecies' occurred well after the calamity took place. The same reasoning applies to gospel versions of Jesus' instructions to his disciples when he sent them out to proclaim the good news and warned them of terrible persecution. In fact, there was no question of persecution at the time—and certainly not from 'governors and kings' in bucolic Galilee.³ The gospel writers were simply updating the message so that it applied to their own time and using Jesus as the mouthpiece. This is not to say that the momentum of theological thought (such as it is) has been allowed to filter down from the rarefied atmosphere of academe into the lay community—or even that the laity would want to know—but at least among the intelligentsia the foundation has been laid for understanding the mythic elements of the Jesus story.

There has, however, arisen a point beyond which none of the modern apologies will pass. It is the acceptance of Jesus' powers as a healer. The more conservative retain the view that the 'cures' were effected by some supra-natural power which Jesus, as the Son of God, possessed. The modern rationalists hold that the faith Jesus was able to inspire in his patients by the power of his presence allowed them in effect to cure themselves. The power of faith, they would say, is itself a mighty force for good.

Unquestionably, the exploration of the human mind is incomplete and a great deal has yet to be explained. But the so-called evidence of the efficacy of faith healing is notoriously unreliable. Put more correctly, there are liars, damned liars, and there are faith healers.

The Jews were oppressed, their freedom inhibited by a ruler who had alienated himself from them. Plans for his assassination were rife. Violent bloodshed was common place. The people's mood swayed from hopelessness to rage to despair. The air was alive with rumour and portent of all kinds.

In such an atmosphere the news of a new faith healer breaks like a wave over the population and reports of his deeds spread rapidly. They appear on all sides instantaneously and in the receding tide the supplicants rush to meet him. And they come not just from the uneducated mass but from every social rank (and for some reason beyond the scope of this work, women seem to lead the vanguard). Adulation is showered indiscriminately upon the healer himself. Much as he would protest—and Jesus often did—that the power to heal came not from himself but from some higher authority, the adulation is nevertheless invested in the person of the healer. Much as he might try to resist it, the effect is to inflate the ego of the healer to monstrous proportions and to produce a vision of himself as a figure of mysterious grandeur.

It is a condition often observed in politicians. It is a form of inner corruption and mental delusion. But in the politician—with some notable exceptions—the symptoms are relatively mild compared to the effect upon the faith healer. And this is true even when the faith healer knows that his 'operations' and 'cures' are effected by sleight of hand and fraudulent 'demonstrations'. As will be seen, Jesus was by no means immune to its effects.

Notes

1. Strauss.
2. The first and most spectacular example is that of Moses and the manna in the wilderness. Jesus could not be seen to be less efficacious in such matters. Elijah's feeding of the 5,000 is another obvious parallel.
3. Matthew 10:16-19.

9

The Disciples

ACCORDING to all the gospels, before Jesus began his ministry he set about attracting a group of disciples to his cause. As has been noted, the Talmud refers to only five disciples and in fact only the most minor changes would need to be made to the gospels if the Talmud were accurate. The only disciples who receive more than passing mention in the synoptics are Peter, his brother Andrew, the brothers James and John and Judas Iscariot, the son of Simon the Zealot, also a disciple.

The identity of the twelve differs a little among the synoptics as does Jesus' method of recruiting them. In the first chapter of Mark, directly after Jesus' baptism by John and the Baptist's subsequent arrest, Jesus is back in Galilee preaching when, passing by the waterfront at the Sea of Galilee, he sees one Simon and his brother Andrew. He calls to them, tells them he will make them 'fishers of men' and they follow immediately. A little further along he sees John and James, the sons of Zebedee, mending their nets. He calls to them and they come along also.

For some time these four are his only disciples. But then after a preaching tour he goes up into the hills and calls 'to those whom he desired'. He appoints another eight to travel with him, to preach, and to have authority to cast out demons. The new recruits are Philip, Bartholomew, Matthew, Thomas, another James (son of Alphaeus), Thaddeus, Simon the Canaanite, and Judas Iscariot.

Essentially, Matthew's version is the same as Mark's and almost certainly has been taken from the earlier book—the only real difference being the extent of the preaching tour which Jesus undertakes with the four original disciples before calling the others to him. Matthew inserts many of the more famous sermons, parables and miracles in this period. The author also reveals that Matthew is a tax collector. Jesus' instructions to the twelve are more comprehensive in this gospel; in addition to exorcism they are enjoined to heal the sick, cleanse lepers and, for good measure, 'raise the dead'.[1]

Perceiving the obvious weaknesses in his fellow synoptists' narratives, Luke follows his abiding inclination to round out the story and give the disciples some semblance of motivation for throwing up their work and following the preacher. According to the third gospel, Jesus first meets Simon whom he calls Peter when Simon beseeches him to cure his mother-in-law of a high fever. By this time Jesus has been preaching long enough to have gained a reputation for his cures. And he is successful in curing Simon's mother-in-law. Jesus stands over her and 'rebukes' the fever; the good lady rises immediately and serves them food and drink.

Not long afterwards, Jesus preaches from Simon's boat which is moored a little way from shore. The sermon over, he tells Simon to 'put out into the deep and let your nets down for a catch'. Simon is sceptical: 'Master, we toiled all night and took nothing.' But he does as requested and hauls in a great catch. He is overcome. 'Depart from me for I am a sinful man, O Lord,' he says.

Equally astonished are James and John, the sons of Zebedee who in Luke are Simon's partners. 'Do not be afraid,' says Jesus, 'henceforth you will be catching men.'[2] When they land they leave everything and follow him.

But the incident apparently exhausted Luke's powers of invention because later, while travelling, Jesus sees a tax collector named Levi sitting at the tax office. Out of the blue he calls, '"Follow me," and he left everything and rose and followed him.' When Luke names the disciples there is no mention of Levi so presumably Jesus has changed his name to Matthew. Luke identifies the other additions as Philip, Bartholomew, Thomas, James (the son of Alphaeus), Simon (now the Zealot), Judas Iscariot and another Judas identified as 'the son of James', though which James is not clear.

As usual, the fourth gospel tells a completely different story. When Jesus first appears in John he is at the Jordan where John the Baptist has drawn a large crowd. The Baptist is standing with two of his own disciples and, seeing Jesus walk by, says: 'Behold, the Lamb of God.' The two overhear him and immediately desert their Teacher to follow Jesus. One of them is Andrew, the brother of Simon Peter, and after going to the place where Jesus is staying and speaking with him Andrew is convinced that he is the Messiah they have been searching for. He seeks out his brother who is also impressed and joins the group.

The following day, Jesus decides to go to Galilee but before doing so he 'finds' Philip and says to him, 'Follow me,' which Philip does. Philip in turn 'finds' one Nathanael (unmentioned in the synoptics) and says to him, 'We have found him of whom Moses in the Law and also the prophets wrote, Jesus of Nazareth, the son of Joseph.'

Nathanael is not impressed. 'Can anything good come out of Nazareth?' he asks.

There follows a meeting between him and Jesus which exhibits a flash of humour, a rare thing indeed in Christian literature. Jesus sees Nathanael coming. 'Behold,' he says, 'an Israelite indeed, in whom there is no guile!'

Nathanael: 'How do you know me?'

Jesus: 'Before Philip called you, when you were under the fig tree, I saw you.'

Nathanael (scoffing?): 'Rabbi, you are the Son of God! You are the King of Israel!'

Jesus (smiling?): 'Because I said to you I saw you under the fig tree, do you believe? You shall see greater things than these.'

Nathanael's reply is not recorded and Jesus continues (more seriously now?): 'Truly, truly, I say to you, you will see heaven opened and the angels of God ascending and descending upon the son of man.'[3]

There the passage ends and John goes on to the first miracle, but Nathanael duly joined the band.

Though he asserts that Jesus was accompanied by twelve disciples, John mentions specifically (in addition to his original four) only Judas Iscariot (son of Simon Iscariot), another Judas, Thomas (called The Twin), the sons of Zebedee and the Beloved Disciple (who is never named).

It is worth recalling that the gospels are in no sense objective representations of the life of their central figure. As has been seen already, the early life of Jesus in the synoptics is, to say the least, sketchy, and no real attempt has been made to get to the truth of the matter. The same applies to the accounts of the disciples.

It is quite absurd to suggest—as in Mark and Matthew—that Jesus simply walked along the Galilean shore and selected a few fishermen who, without a word passing between them, suddenly felt impelled to throw up their occupations and leave their wives and their families to follow him. There is no evidence whatever that Jesus exerted some supernatural power over them which instantly convinced them of his messianic identity. On the contrary, he is often forced to berate them for their lack of faith.

It is possible to feel some sympathy for the storyteller in Luke in his desire to lay a foundation for the disciples' decision, but none at all for the method he chose. He simply combined a current legend, repeated with variations in John, of a great haul of fish caught at Jesus' direction, with the 'cure' of Peter's mother-in-law from a later section in Matthew.

On the whole the version in the fourth gospel is more plausible. The exchanges between Jesus and his prospective disciples Andrew, Simon and particularly Nathanael, have a ring of authenticity, of eyewitness reportage. They give a picture of a crowded encampment on the banks of the Jordan, of impassioned groupings, instant allegiances wrought in the excitement of religious expectation, of gurus contending for a following from the ranks of the susceptible pilgrims. It is the most natural place imaginable for Jesus to have secured his most energetic disciples.

How fortuitous it would have seemed to the disciples to have discovered a Teacher from their own region but with wisdom and sophistication carved from an experience of life – and perhaps a period of intense study in an Essene community – which they themselves had never known. How natural it would be for them to be attracted to such a figure, slightly in awe of his sense of authority but proud in the knowledge that he was one of their own.

Another interesting element of the fourth gospel version is the connection it establishes between Jesus and John the Baptist, a relationship which all the gospels agree was of great significance throughout Jesus' public ministry.

The Baptist was a very considerable personage at the time. Dressed in camel's hide secured by a rough leather belt, eating locusts and wild honey and crying imprecations from the wilderness, John was a prophet in the mould of the most venerated figures of Israel's religious history, a direct successor to Amos and Jeremiah and even, some said, Elijah himself. Was not his call to repentance the same command from Yahweh's messenger heard so often before from the Saints of old? Did he not establish himself on the Jordan at the very place Elijah ascended to heaven with a multitude of angels? Was it not said that before the Messiah would arise, another would precede him to herald his coming? Or was he, perhaps, the long-awaited Messiah himself?

Small wonder that he attracted such crowds and that his utterances had so great an influence upon the people. Indeed, one sect, the Mandaeans, came to venerate him as the True Prophet and to dismiss Jesus as a false Messiah. Their descendants retain the faith in an area of Syria to this day.

The Baptist himself seems not to have claimed to be the Messiah, though we are dependent on the gospels for this information and they would be most unlikely to report it if he had. Moreover, it would not have been expected of him to verbally articulate the claim. Traditionally, the prophets made their statements by the manner of their coming, by actions rather than words.[4] John's style of dress, his spurning of creature comforts, his symbolic baptism, were the syllables of his message and they were quite as powerful as any overt proclamation.

Indeed to declare oneself the Messiah was a highly dangerous act for two quite separate reasons. The Romans were not greatly concerned with the subtleties of Jewish disputation about the true role of the Messiah—whether he would come in the form of a warrior king or a priestly redeemer. If he disturbed the civil order he was automatically a threat and would be treated accordingly.

Just as importantly, if the declaration was actually enunciated by the putative Messiah and he failed to live up to Jewish expectations, his end would be quick. That had happened before. It would happen again, many times.

THE JUDEAN DISCIPLES

It has become accepted Christian teaching over the centuries that Jesus' disciples were confined to the Galilean twelve. However, there is strong evidence in the gospels that he also acquired a small following in and around Jerusalem. Included among these are Nicodemus, Joseph of Arimathea, Lazarus and his sisters Mary and Martha, and the Beloved Disciple himself.

The synoptics underplay the role this group performed in the final act of Jesus' life, and given the books' Galilean focus this is not surprising. It is clear that Jesus made little or no attempt to integrate the two groups, and his reasons were probably sound. The rough, illiterate fishermen of Galilee would have little in common with the wealthy, cultivated Joseph of Arimathea and still less with the Beloved Disciple who seems to have been well connected at the Temple and who is pictured repeatedly as 'lying close to the breast of Jesus'. Also, it is the mark of a leader in all ages to keep the left hand in ignorance of the right's activities, to direct his forces in such a way that only he knows the total picture.

It is not surprising either that orthodox scholars should have shied away from the questions raised by the role of the Judean disciples. To accord them any significance at all would be to destroy the comfortable symmetry of the synoptics and produce questions for which they provide no plausible answers.

If, as the synoptics assert, for example, Jesus visited Jerusalem only once during his ministry—and then at the dramatic conclusion of his life—how did he establish a bond with Nicodemus and Joseph of Arimathea which clearly pre-dated his arrival in the city? Who arranged for the ass which he would ride into the city to be tethered and waiting for him on the outskirts and who were they who gave it to his Galilean disciples on request? Who lent him the house in which they celebrated the Last Supper? How could he have known Mary and Martha of nearby Bethany with whom he spent each night of the final week of his life? Who was the Beloved Disciple?

For these questions to be answered logically, it is clear that Jesus must have spent time in and around Jerusalem, a fact which is not recorded in the synoptics. The only real question is whether this occurred during his ministry or before the baptism in the Jordan which the gospels say signalled the start of his public life.

The timetable of the synoptics suggests that Jesus' ministry lasted for not much more than a year. Many Christian scholars hold the view that this is too short a time to accomplish all the travelling and all the preaching indicated by the books themselves, particularly Matthew and Luke. No one has suggested that in addition the entourage made a trip to Jerusalem which they all overlooked. Accordingly, some exegetes favour the three-year time span indicated by John in which Jesus celebrates no fewer than three Passovers, the first and third in Jerusalem and the second in the hills of Galilee.

But unfortunately the version in John is not very persuasive. According to John, during the first Passover Jesus attacks the moneychangers in the Temple and drives them out. Also, it is then that he speaks of the destruction of the Temple and his capacity to raise it again in three days. In the synoptics these activities are two of the triggers which enrage the Temple hierarchy who have him arrested and brought to trial. It seems hardly likely that the authorities were simply recalling these activities three years later when the arrest was made.

Then there is the tendency of the author of John to use a whole series of feasts as springboards for sermonising—the more the better. If he can string them out to a Feast of the Tabernacles, a Feast for an unnamed purpose, a Feast of the Dedication (none of which are mentioned in the synoptics) and three Passovers, he is able to give full vent to his threats and imprecations. If John is to be believed, Jesus spent more time during the three years at feasts in Jerusalem than he did in Galilee.

There seem to be two possibilities: either Jesus made a secret trip to Jerusalem without the Galilean disciples, or he found followers there prior to the beginning of the ministry.

At first glance there would appear to be problems with the secret journey alternative. The Galilean disciples are pictured as being so constant a part of his entourage that it is difficult to conceive of him without them. But in fact the synoptics do provide an excellent opportunity for just such a trip. All say quite specifically that at a point in his ministry he sent the twelve away from him 'two by two' to preach on his behalf. His instructions are detailed and the version in Mark is typical:

He charged them to take nothing for their journey except a staff; no bread, no bag, no money in their belts; but to wear sandals and not to put on two tunics. And he said to them: 'Where you enter a house, stay there until you leave the place. And if any place will not receive you and they refuse to hear you, when you leave shake off the dust that is on your feet for a testimony against them.' So they went out and preached that men should repent. And they cast out many demons, and anointed with oil many that were sick and healed them.[5]

No mention is made of Jesus' own activities while his companions are away, but the indications in Mark are that there would have been plenty of time for him to journey to Jerusalem if he were so inclined. Indeed, there was probably good reason for him to be out of Galilee at the time, as will be seen when his mission is examined in narrative.

There is no direct evidence in any of the gospels for Jesus having been in Jerusalem prior to the 'official' beginning of his ministry. But it is clear from the early chapters of John that by the time he recruited the Galilean disciples by the Jordan he was already a practising Teacher. Moreover, there are indications in the synoptics that when he began to preach in Nazareth it was as a hometown boy who had gone away and achieved a measure of success before returning to bring his message to his own people. The congregations in the synagogues listen to him for a while as to any visiting preacher before someone recognises him and they are surprised, or, as Matthew would have it, 'astonished'.

'Where did this man get this wisdom and these mighty works? Is not this the carpenter's son? Is not his mother called Mary? And are not his brothers James and Joseph and Simon and Judas? And are not all his sisters with us? Where then did this man get all this?'[6]

Apparently he has learned to read and he clothes himself in 'authority' and speaks with a scholarly perspective quite foreign to that of the carpenter's boy they had known as a youth. That they then proceed to reject him is a beautifully human (and oft-repeated) response. It has the ring of total authenticity.

It seems therefore that both the secret journey and the pre-Jordan sojourn are more than possible and the acceptance of one in no way precludes the other. On the contrary, Jesus would be far more likely to leave Galilee during his ministry for a solitary, brief journey to Jerusalem if he already had friends and followers there.

Because of the reticence of the synoptics, little is known of the individual personalities of the Judean disciples. It is necessary to rely on the fourth gospel.

John says that Nicodemus was 'a man of the Pharisees, a ruler of the Jews', and there the description ends. In the first instance he and Jesus meet 'by night' and Nicodemus questions him about the capacity of an old man to be 'born again'.

'Can he enter a second time into his mother's womb and be born?' he asks.

Jesus instructs the Pharisee on the meaning of the term and they part inconclusively. However, three years later (reckoning from John) Nicodemus faithfully accompanies Joseph to the crucifixion.

All four gospels name Joseph of Arimathea in this connection and both John and Matthew are quite unequivocal in designating him a disciple. All are agreed that he is a rich man and Mark and Luke indicate that he is a respected member of 'the council'. This may not have been the Sanhedrin as is sometimes taught since the members of that body voted unanimously for the conviction of Jesus. Rather, he could have been a member of the secular town council in Jerusalem. Little more is known of him and after his one brief but highly important appearance he disappears from the New Testament altogether.

Joseph of Arimathea has a long history in later apocryphal literature, much of it centring on his possession of the so-called Holy Grail, the goblet supposedly used by Jesus and the disciples during the Last Supper. But this has no basis in fact.

Mary, Martha and their brother Lazarus who lived in nearby Bethany also figure significantly in the last chapter of Jesus' life. Indeed, according to John it is Jesus' raising of Lazarus from the dead which precipitates his capture and trial by the Temple authorities. Mary and Martha appear in both Luke and John as two sisters who dote on Jesus and the story is told in both gospels of Mary anointing Jesus with costly oil. It is clear from similar stories in the other gospels that this relationship was a quite vital factor in the denouement of Jesus' story. In fact Matthew credits the incident as the cause of Judas Iscariot's decision to betray Jesus into the hands of the Temple guards.

THE BELOVED DISCIPLE

Thus, to one of the most intriguing figures in the gospels, the Beloved Disciple. He is never named and only so designated in

John though there is a glimpse of him in Mark as the young man almost captured with Jesus in Gethsemane. On that occasion, in Mark's graphic words, 'a young man followed him (Jesus) with nothing but a linen cloth about his body; and they seized him, but he left the linen cloth and ran away naked'.[7]

The Beloved Disciple is presented always as an alluring, sensuous figure (and certainly none of the Galilean disciples would fit that description), most often lying close to the breast of Jesus during the Last Supper.[8]

Some exegetes have suggested that he is the invention of a group of editors who worked on the Johannine gospel and no doubt this would be a useful way of disposing of an embarrassing problem. However, most scholars agree that John's version of the trial of Jesus could only have come from an eyewitness or someone privy to the recollections of a witness. No one has suggested that these anonymous editors could possibly have fulfilled such criteria.

On the other hand there is the tradition that the Beloved Disciple was present at the trial and that his first-hand recollections were used by the Elder of Ephesus in compiling the gospel.

The likelihood is that he was a young priest at the time, familiar with the physical geography of the Temple as well as the inner workings of its institutions. This alone would have allowed him to be present at the trial and to record it in some detail. It is also likely that it was the Beloved Disciple's house which Jesus used for the Last Supper. This would explain his presence at the meal as well as his place of honour at the table on the right hand of Jesus—two points which equally militate against the house belonging to either Nicodemus or Joseph of Arimathea, neither of whom was present.

It must be noted that no reference is made in the synoptics to the presence there of the Beloved Disciple. But given the jealousy and jostling for preferment within the band perhaps the omission is understandable. The Last Supper and the events surrounding it became the focal point of early Christian worship. It would be the most natural and human of reactions for the Galileans to erase from their accounts the presence of a wealthy young priest, a Jew, who seemed to count for more than they in Jesus' affections.

JUDAS

The position of Judas Iscariot in the framework of discipleship has always been a problem for Christian apologists. Stated simply, the dilemma has been this: if Jesus knew all along that Judas would betray him, why did he call him as a disciple? And if the betrayal was inevitable, why should Jesus have condemned the man so viciously? Even if Jesus became aware of his intention only shortly before the act, why did he not make some attempt to stop Judas? Again, why condemn Judas so roundly?[9] Surely, in both instances, by his very inactivity Jesus became a party to the act.

The answer to this dilemma is quite central to the Christian message and deserves to be dealt with in some detail. But at present it is only necessary to suggest, upon the evidence, the relationship which existed between them.

In the gospels Judas is always placed last in any list of the disciples, for obvious reasons. But equally obviously, this is no indication of the place he occupied in the pecking order of intimacy with the Master during Jesus' ministry. In fact, what meagre evidence there is suggests quite the contrary. According to all accounts, he was the treasurer of the group, concerned not only with their own support but with the distribution of funds to the poor and needy.

Some exegetes have suggested that this was the lowliest job he could have been offered in the entourage of one who had so little care for worldly goods. And it cannot be denied that Jesus preached against the spiritual and moral disabilities of wealth and on occasion of the virtues of poverty. However, this is a quite separate concern from Jesus' responsibilities as the leader of a relatively large group of dependants, and there are indications that the sums involved were by no means inconsiderable. For in addition to the male disciples he was accompanied by a number of women including, according to Luke: 'Mary, called Magdalene, from whom seven demons had been cast out, and Joanna, the wife of Chuza, Herod's steward, and Suzanna, and many others who provided for them out of their means'.[10]

This passage is interesting in itself for the light it throws on the real composition of the entourage as opposed to the picture preferred by Christian image-makers who have portrayed the group as a band of twelve penurious ascetics following their leader in hardship over the harsh byways of Palestine. But its significance here is clear. Women from as exalted a position as Joanna were wealthy in their own right and if, as Luke says, there were many of them, the funds available to Jesus and Judas for distribution must have been quite large.

In those circumstances, his appointment as treasurer reveals an intimacy between the two which other disciples did not share. His position would have allowed him direct and private access to the Master.

It is apparent, too, that Judas is a young man and almost certainly a highly emotional one. He is described in John as the son of another disciple (Simeon or Simon) whom Luke designates 'the Zealot' and nothing in the other accounts refutes this description. The Zealots were active in both Galilee and Jerusalem and, as a member of the sect, Judas would have the necessary contacts in the capital to guide Jesus and provide shelter on visits there. He would have been the logical member of the group for Jesus to employ as a liaison between the two sets of followers. Whether this occurred in fact is, of course, speculative. But, as will be seen, if Judas were the go-between, it was the least of the duties he carried out on Jesus' behalf.

Notes

1. Matthew 10:8.
2. Luke 5:4-11.
3. John 1:46-51.
4. For example, at the time of the Babylonian invasion, Jeremiah walked about the streets of Jerusalem with a yoke on his neck symbolising his demands that the Jews submit to Nebuchadnezzar.
5. Mark 6:8-13.
6. Matthew 13:55-56.
7. Mark 14:51-52.
8. John 13:23-25; 19:26; 20:2-10; 21:7; 21:20-24.
9. Mark 14:21.
10. Luke 8:2-3.

PART 3

The Narrative

10

The Man

BEFORE embarking on the study of Jesus' public ministry it is necessary to pause and consider the man himself. Who was this Nazarene who would arouse such devotion and such enmity in both Galilee and Jerusalem? What were the forces within which impelled him to forgo the comfortable obscurity of his town and trade for the hazardous vocation of religious messenger in a land fervent with spiritual and political passion?

Unquestionably, the circumstances which produced these motivating forces were traumatic—powerful enough to compel the man to walk away from his family, to seek the adoration of the crippled, the epileptic and the insane. They drove him to see himself as the chosen messenger of Yahweh, the instrument of God, the herald of the end of the world and in the end they demanded that he volunteer himself for the terrible ordeal of crucifixion.

One of the problems in answering these questions is that over the centuries deduction and intelligent speculation concerning the birth and the so-called missing years of Jesus' life have not been regarded as a respectable intellectual endeavour. It is an attitude which has robbed the quest for an historical Jesus of much of its meaning.

It is simply illogical to attempt to understand the course of his life and the cause of his death, the essence of his message and the truth or otherwise of the gospel accounts, without first forming a cogent view of the internal forces which obsessed and propelled the man. Yet this is precisely what has happened. Learned theologians and exegetes have dispelled this area from their minds and have concentrated on the barren controversies raised by the obvious contradictions in the received texts.

It is admitted that the battleground for 'respectable' argument was delineated in an era which lacked psychoanalytical foundation. It is understandable that scholars in the 18th and 19th centuries were hesitant about venturing into a world without recognisable signposts. And given the quintessentially conservative nature of religionists it is not surprising—though it is shameful—that few, if any, have yet found the courage to do so in the 20th century.

But to understand such a compulsion as Jesus possessed it is necessary to return to his very beginnings, the foundation upon which his life was built: his birth.

Some of the suspicious circumstances of the birth have already been noted:

- The assertion by Matthew and Luke that the conception took place outside wedlock and the anger of Joseph at the discovery of his fiancée's condition.
- The account in the Koran of the 'full-grown man' who forced his attentions upon Mary and her fear of the disgrace which would follow.
- The bald statement of the Talmud alleging Jesus' illegitimacy and the naming of the soldier accused of being the father.
- The reported departure of the parents from their home town for a long journey prior to the birth.

By itself such evidence falls well short of proof, but more follows quickly. There is the constant and continuing animosity between himself and his family in all his public utterances. His mother and brothers are spurned, his legal father ignored or cuttingly disparaged. He places himself apart from them and the feeling, it seems, is reciprocated, at least until he has gained a measure of public recognition. These are the actions of a man with an abiding insecurity about his own beginnings, of one who has been told by one parent or the other or even by the cruel children of the town repeating the hateful gossip of their elders—of the scandal which surrounded his birth.[1]

It takes no special insight or imagination to picture such a child, his ears ringing with the taunts of the neighbourhood brats, pouring out his heart to his mother and seeking her comfort and reassurance. It takes no special sensitivity on the child's part for him to hear the shouts and sneers again as a youth, to question again and to see the awful truth reflected in his father's eyes, to carry that moment to the darkness of his bed and to lie sleepless until it all falls into place—his father's unguarded outbursts over the years, painful words which only now become comprehensible; his mother's quiver of fear, the sudden moistness of her hand as Roman soldiers approach; the ill-disguised contempt shown her by the holier-than-thou wives of snobbish Pharisees; his parents' obvious preferment of his younger brothers…and always, the terrible memory of his father's face as he turns away from the son's anxious questioning.

It is an intimate human drama repeated a thousand times before and since, though never with such far-reaching consequences.

To a Galilean boy whose own private world is suddenly torn apart, the present must have seemed an insurmountable ordeal. The next day, the next month, the mute accusation suddenly visible on the faces of his friends and the older folk who surrounded him with their graceless puritanism, these were the great obstacles which confronted and tortured him. And his family: how could he continue to live with them to whom his very existence was a reminder of their disgrace?

If such were the circumstances, it is hardly surprising that the child, stripped of his security, and overwhelmed by a combination of worthlessness and guilt, should have reacted in the way that Jesus did.

In his guilt he lashed out at them, spurned them and retreated inside himself to build a new framework for his life, a new private world where his existence would acquire a sense of worth, something—anything—to sustain its continuance.

His resources were few. He was unlettered, poor and unskilled, but for his carpentry his father was teaching him and which was suddenly repugnant to him, a member of a subject people, a northerner, a bastard. But there was within him a driving force, a power which he did not completely comprehend. It was part of him yet at times it felt separate, a compulsive restlessness, a spiritual sense which he sometimes identified with God.

There was the quickness of his mind, and as the moods passed, the speed with which he was able to defend himself from the verbal assaults of his peers.

There was the name he had nourished in his heart from his earliest recollections. Yesu'a, 'The Help of Yahweh'. It returned now to comfort him and to turn his mind to the Law and to the words of the prophets.

His religion was doubly useful for it seemed, as for so many of his fellow Jews, to provide the only possible escape from the oppression of the hated Roman overlords. As a ten-year-old he had seen the gathering of the rebels under the great Judas of Gamala and rejoiced with all the other boys as his men struggled to throw off the yoke of bondage. But in no time at all, it seemed, the uprising was hammered into the dust of Galilee and once again the futility of earthly struggle was driven home.

We may speculate that the need for escape grew into a passion. The workshop became a prison and at every opportunity he would break clear of it to walk alone through the grainfields and the pasture lands of the Galilean countryside. At times he would join a crowd of villagers to watch from the outskirts the performance of a travelling wonder worker as he exorcised the sinful demons of disease. On other occasions he would stop to listen as a wandering Rabbi spoke of the great hope, the Messiah, who would deliver Israel from its oppression, and he would thrill with the rest of the believers at such a wondrous thought.

But the time most precious was that which he spent alone, bent in thought, searching for the source of his power, struggling to find an identity which seemed just out of reach. It was a time to reflect on the world and his own place in it, on the variegated scenes his first tentative steps into the wider sphere presented for his understanding.

He would remember the distaste with which the Pharisees treated the faith healer and, more especially, the lowly and the crippled to whom he gave hope and even a measure of joy. He would find a strange sense of identity with the supplicants. He was, after all, a cripple himself, also a victim, and he would feel an overwhelming compassion for the pariahs, his emotional kin, as they sought release from their afflictions. And at the same time and unbidden, he would stoke the fires of hatred for their accusers which would later burst forth in uncontrolled flames of abuse and threats of damnation 'where men will weep and gnash their teeth' unparalleled in their cruelty.[2]

A divided soul—both lover and hater—he would walk until surrounded by darkness seeking some way to meld the two halves. On his return home and in answer to the shouts and the demands of a father who was fast becoming a stranger he would retreat inside himself. Perhaps as he prepared to sleep he would remember the healer, and the self-confidence and inner strength which seemed to flow from the man to the eager supplicants in the crowd as their hands reached out toward him. And he would know that in that need there resided an unquenchable love.

To such a child as he grew to manhood the restrictions of his small town would become intolerable. His concerns were not their concerns, his vision ranged beyond them, and beyond even Galilee to Jerusalem itself—not the Jerusalem of the Passover ritual, where people crowded in tents outside the city or in bare, ill-kept rooms cheek by jowl with other pilgrims to offset the inflated prices the Judeans reserved for their northern brethren. No, the Jerusalem he sought was the cauldron of disputation and feverish expectancy—for there and only there would the Messiah declare himself and be revealed. He craved the Jerusalem which would meet and match his restlessness, which would instruct him in the wider world, which would listen to his teeming thoughts and see him for what he was, not the bastard son of a carpenter but an individual with his own desperate needs and a great well of love and compassion dammed within, seeking only the moment for its release.

Perhaps the family held firm. Whatever the circumstances of his birth, he was the eldest and only the eldest could assume the mantle of responsibility should the head of the household die. The alternative was to admit the shame publicly. As the first born, Yesu'a must stay.

But then, perhaps not. Perhaps it was the time of ultimate rejection, the time for an arrangement mutually agreed upon, which would allow Yesu'a to follow his own inclinations and seek the great destiny which he claimed awaited him far away from the town of his childhood, and install his nearest brother, Joses (Joseph) as the second-in-command. That way everyone would benefit. The wanderer would be appeased and the family's future stabilised. And as a bonus, twenty years of embarrassment would depart with him. An excellent arrangement all round but for one terrible consequence: deep inside, a twenty-year-old soul would be subjected once again to the trauma of rejection.

Two things sustained him. The first was the intimacy he was beginning to feel with that power within him, 'the Essence of the Most High'. There was a growing communion. He ascribed to it all his finest impulses, all the compassion and sympathy he sought to share with the unfortunates of the earth, all the aspirations of his countrymen seeking spiritual release from the heathen bondage, all the filial love denied its normal outlet by the circumstances of his birth.

The other was the concept so beloved by the Essenes of the End of the Days with its messianic figure heralding the new world order. It was at once the prospect of an end to his own personal torture and inner shame, and a new world where the values of the old were inverted and the poor, the meek, the outcast found the highest joy Jesus could imagine—the bliss of being enclosed for all eternity in the arms of a loving father. Within this concept he could find a panacea for all his afflictions and it is not surprising that he should begin a search or even a preparation for the central figure in the drama, the Messiah around which it all revolved, as soon as he was able.

To support himself on his journey to the community, Jesus had his trade; there was always work for an itinerant carpenter. But carpentry could not have been satisfying. It provided him with mobility but it could not feed the spiritual and emotional hunger inside. For that he needed a different environment, one devoted entirely to the world of the spirit, an organisation which would enclose him physically and give him the paternal security which comes only from a voluntary subjugation to a higher discipline.

Among the alternatives open to him, the Essenes were the most congenial to his needs. Within an Essenic settlement and its communal ethic (which would become so much a part of the early Christian Church) he could find that security.

There would also be an opportunity to supplement his early, haphazard Pharisaic education. With his new facility the old gospels would open to him and the words of the prophets bite into his mind and excite his imagination. He would learn the mysteries of exorcism and through the faith healer's art prepare himself in a practical way to help the maimed and the demented, and their love would reach out to him.

But perhaps most importantly he would learn of the character of the Messiah, the figure which stood at the centre of Essenic thought. So concentrated was their vision of him that at times it seemed to fragment the Anointed One, as though not all the qualities demanded of him could co-exist in a single personality. There was a Teacher of Righteousness, founder of the sect who lived and died more than a century ago. Perhaps somehow he would return to lead a spiritual mission. There was another, a Warrior King, whose concerns would be temporal, whose great achievement would be the expulsion of the physical heathen presence (Roman and Greek) from the Holy Land.

However, it was a fluid conception. In both cases there was a capacity for interpretation. Leaders among the communities and individuals within them could build their own conception of the Messiah without violence to their allegiance to the group. Only when the divergence between group and individual lengthened to the point where the one became an irrelevance to the other did they part company.

That this occurred in Jesus' case, and, if it did, how long the process took, can only be postulated. There is no hard evidence to support it, only the deep similarities between many of Jesus' own attitudes and those of the Essenes. But on one vital issue the division between them is complete. The Essenes believed that in the hierarchy of the New Kingdom they, the Saints, would occupy a favoured position among the Elect (Israel itself). By their asceticism, their purity, by their strict adherence to the Law, they had earned such a place in the Kingdom of God. They deserved it. Their renunciation of the world and its sinful ways itself proclaimed their worth.

This concept was abhorrent to Jesus. It meant that ritual took precedence. It meant that the self-righteous Pharisees and their supercilious wives would again hold a position of favour. It meant that the rich Sadducees, simply by observing the letter of the Law, could buy their preferment in the Kingdom of God. It meant that the pariahs and the outcasts—his own kind—crippled by earthly circumstance, would continue to suffer the barbed oppression of their 'betters' for all time. It meant that Yahweh could not see beyond the form by which men publicise their piety into the truth of their hearts. It meant that the essence of God within him did not share his flood tide of compassion.

He knew that to be wrong; inconceivable. He knew his God. He knew the love He bore for the weak and the maimed who sought release from their pain in the wine of oblivion, and in the great expectation.

He shared the latter. Soon his accusers would claim he relished the former.

It may well have been that Jesus first heard the name of John, later to be called The Baptist, as a fellow Essene. It is even possible that he left the sect to follow John as a disciple, hopeful that he had found the promised Messiah. All that is known for certain in the gospels' telling is that at a particular stage Jesus was attracted to the Baptist and, directly following his association with him, he began his own ministry. Moreover, there is another possibility more attuned to the known chronology of events: that before he made contact with the Baptist his footsteps led him to the physical core of his spiritual yearnings—Jerusalem.

The importance of that city to a Jew obsessed with the spirit could hardly be overestimated. From his earliest days he had known it to be the fulcrum of his religion, the temporal evidence of God's ancient compact with His chosen people, the home of the covenant. It was here, surely, that the good news of the Messiah's arrival would first find voice. It is unthinkable that he should not have been drawn to its teeming streets, its excited, expectant pilgrims, its piety and its depravity.

Strengthened by the instruction he had absorbed at the hands of the Essenes, his guttural northern accent refined a little by his travels and by his association with the learned men of the commune, his mind fired by the certain knowledge that the End of the Days approached—perhaps here for the first time, the young mystic raised his voice to the multitude and bid them come nearer.

There was about him an intensity, a strength of will born of a terrible need, which caused passers-by to check their steps and stay a moment with him before hurrying about their business. Some stayed longer and listened to his message, crude and malformed as yet but nevertheless steeped with portent. One or two remained at the end and afterwards perhaps sought his company and offered him the hospitality of their homes.

Among these could well have been men of affairs like Joseph of Arimathea and Nicodemus; rich men who had heard from the young preacher the hopelessness of their estate in the world to come, the impossibility of their ever attaining a place in heaven without first renouncing their wealth and their pious arrogance. They had heard him say they must be 'reborn'. They must know more, the formula, quickly, before the apocalypse descended.

But as well as his dealings with the rich there was another element in Jesus' message and in his character which may well have found expression in Jerusalem at the time. It was an attitude which, more than any other, would undermine his capacity to inspire the great mass of the Jewish people to follow him and to accept him as the promised Messiah.

It was his predilection for the company of sinners.[3] Not the poor and the crippled to whom he was able to offer hope in the inverted values of the world to come, but a quite separate group, the moral degenerates of society. The harlots, the publicans, the tax collectors, the homosexuals—they were people set adrift from the mainstream by their moral proclivities, who exerted a special fascination upon Jesus. Time and again throughout his ministry he would be drawn to them and they to him. He would seek out a tax collector, the most despised of men, so deeply corrupt that the orthodox Church offered him no way back from his damnation, and offer him a place in his company. He would dine with harlots, accept into his group runaway wives, so conduct himself that his adversaries would be able to pass him off as 'a drunkard and a glutton' and even suggest that he was an instrument of the devil himself.[4]

He would become careless of hygiene, contemptuous of the Sabbath strictures and would be known as the defender of what his contemporaries would brand moral turpitude. He would gather about him a retinue of women camp followers who would 'provide for him from their own means'; he would applaud the public demonstration of affection from a woman in another's house and encourage the sensuous attentions of the Beloved Disciple to the point where Peter would become inflamed with jealousy. He would gather the young Judas into his private and inner circle and exercise so powerful an influence upon him that both would meet their death in consequence.

In Jerusalem, perhaps, Jesus came first to know this nether world of women and men starved like himself for the abundance of affection in childhood which lies at the root of so much adult 'immorality'. Perhaps here he learned that the moral cripple is no more blameworthy than the physically afflicted, that the worth of a human spirit should be judged not for its outward self-righteousness but for its inner depth, the greatness of its need, and the strength and the courage of its capacity to reciprocate. For no one stands in greater need of love than the harlot or the tax collector or the homosexual…except perhaps the preacher, the one who presents himself to the world and risks all in the anguished hope that love will be forthcoming.

It would not be surprising if this mutual attraction first made itself felt in the earliest years of his preaching. On the contrary, no member of the human species is more luminously identifiable to his own kind than the 'unnatural' seeker for love. Recognition would be instantaneous.

Perhaps this was the beginning of the friendship between Jesus and the Beloved Disciple. It would be absurd to be dogmatic about it. The only greater absurdity would be to pretend that their relationship had no history whatever, that the young man who ran naked from Gethsemane and who lay upon the breast of Jesus during the Last Supper was no more than a phantom.

But if, as is suggested, Jesus scored some minor triumphs in Jerusalem and gathered a handful of admirers around him, there is no reason to place his achievement higher than that. Jerusalem was a hard school, the hardest of them all, the graveyard of prophets and preachers from time immemorial. Indeed, it is very possible that this preacher, so vulnerable in his need, should have felt himself rejected once again and have left the city burning with shame for his defeat, enraged at its indifference, crushed by its patronising smirk.[5]

He would not have been aware of the new dimension the experience had provided him, the broadening of his humanity, the new maturity of his vision. It was an achievement in itself.

Jerusalem was no longer alien territory. He knew its geography, its politics, its social structure, its piety and its iniquity.

He had touched it but he had not captured it. He could love it and hate it in a single breath. It had tested him and found him wanting...then. But perhaps the day would come when it would rise to meet him and he would ride through its streets at the head of a great army of the faithful and the city would hang upon his words and acclaim him. He would bend it to his will.

Or was that merely a dream?

There was another, the man they called The Baptist, and every day some new report of his activity would filter through the crowded streets, its meaning interpreted and reinterpreted as it passed from group to group, its significance continually growing until versions separated and found an independent existence of their own. Then they in turn would be pondered and new meanings found until, it seemed, the very air was filled with news of his sayings and deeds.

In Jerusalem and all across Palestine the process repeated itself and people flocked to hear him and to learn the special significance of his baptismal rite. The Romans and the Herodian kings sent spies to learn his intentions. Did he have political aspirations? Could he lead a rebellion?

The Sadducees and the Pharisees of the Sanhedrin sent their own agents. Was he a prophet? Did he claim to be the Messiah? Did he observe the Law of Moses?

The Essenes sent their own delegation. Was he the Teacher of Righteousness reincarnate? Was he the first of the Messiahs or would he take up the fallen crown of David and rouse the people against the overlords?

Individual Rabbis from many corners of the land felt the need to see him for themselves, to weigh his message against their own, to sit at his feet and absorb his instruction, to proclaim him the Anointed One and carry his message away with them to all who would listen.

Among those who came seeking was one Yesu'a, a native of Nazareth, small and dark-complexioned, but with an air of intensity which lent him stature. That he stayed and became a part of the Baptist's circle of disciples seems almost beyond argument. All four gospels record that it was John who initiated Jesus' ministry, though there is no mention in the fourth gospel of the physical act of baptism. (By the time it was written the author found it inconceivable that Jesus would have need of baptism to wash away his sins, however symbolic the act.) All show a continuing dialogue between the two preachers after their parting. Mark and Matthew record that in the first phase of his ministry Jesus' message is almost identical to that of the Baptist: 'Repent, for the Kingdom of God is at hand!'

Perhaps more convincing is that the alternative—of Jesus receiving a Lordly Anointing during the act of baptism as would suddenly transform him into the deified Son of God—not only beggars the imagination but is specifically contradicted time and again in the subsequent account of his mission.

According to Mark, it was only after the Baptist's arrest by Herod Antipas that Jesus left the wilderness (where John was wont to preach) to begin his independent preaching in Galilee. However, there is no indication of the period the two spent in each other's company. Like all the years of Jesus' life to this point the gospels are deficient and the truth may only be glimmered through what Schweitzer called 'the dark lantern'.

But there was an element in John's message which might have been specially tailored to appeal to the Nazarene and to open the wondrous possibility that he himself might be the Messiah all Israel was seeking. According to the gospels John was quite specific in his belief that his task was simply to be the herald of the promised Messiah, the one who would follow and whose sandal John was not even fit to tie. To be constantly in the presence of such an idea is to give it a life of its own, a continuing and deep-seated importance. And if the hearer is already harbouring deep within him the ecstatic possibility that he might be singled out by his Heavenly Father for some great work, the words of John could only be interpreted as an indication, a divine message.

It has been noted that at some point in Jesus' life, prior to the outset of his public ministry, his legal father departed the scene. There is no way of knowing on the present evidence when the old man's death occurred, but it can be assumed that when it did happen it had a profound effect on Jesus. This was the man, after all, who had lent him his name, had provided for him from his earliest years and had been the first figure of authority for him as an infant. The childhood affection was deeply implanted, its effect the more powerfully crystallised because of the later revelation and rejection. The bitterness of their arguments would feed upon it and be fuelled by it and after his departure from the family circle the hateful memories would remain as unwanted companions.

With the news of his death would come the guilt, the regret, the agony of the soul which demanded some form of release, and the need to replace the father figure he had spurned. When it came it did so in the classic manner. It generalised the particular. It buried the personal figure of Joseph deep in the recesses of the unconscious beside the unknown and unknowable natural father, and then projected its need for expiation upon a spiritual concept: the Heavenly Father Yahweh, the creation of Isaiah and Amos and Hosea of the scriptures. It came without volition. In the circumstances of the time and of the man it arrived with a grand inevitability. It was a magnificent escape, for just beyond the prison walls, a single step away, was limitless bliss. In taking that step the boy Yesu'a became the prophet Jesus. In Yahweh he had found his father.[6]

Notes

1. While much of what follows in this chapter must be conjectural, it is based wholly upon the sources listed and particularly on inferences drawn from Jesus' own words and attitudes during his ministry.

2. Matthew 12:1-36.

3. See Hans Kung, On Being a Christian, p. 271.

4. Matthew 12:24.

5. Matthew 23:37-39.

6. Jesus' continuing obsession with the father figure of Yahweh throughout his mission is reflected in the extraordinary amount of space devoted to protestations by him of the paternal relationship. Typical references are Matthew 12:25-30; and John 14:12-31; 15:1-27.

11

The Mission

ACCORDING to Mark, Jesus was fired at the beginning of his ministry (as the Baptist had been) by the prophetic cry which Israel had heard so many times before in her strange, sad history: 'Repent, for the Kingdom of God is at hand'.[1]

Time was short. The End of the Days was imminent. There must be no delay. Israel must be alerted, the nation of the Elect must know that only her act of repentance stood between the hellishness of the Last Days and the bliss of God's Kingdom on earth.

Jesus' mind was aflame with the idea. Nothing would do but that he, Yahweh's appointed messenger, set the entire country blazing with the news.

He would start with his own people, the Galileans, and they would listen to him and begin the great movement which would sweep through the land like a cloud of heavenly locusts to purge it of all its sinful growths. Every resource available to him would be employed to attract their attention. He would speak in the synagogues and in the village squares and by the Sea of Galilee; he would seek out his own kind, the pariahs, the sick at heart, and they would become his vanguard; he would practise the arts of healing so beloved of the masses, but he would take care to distance himself from the cures lest he be seen only as a healer and thus held in contempt by the better educated and more influential members of the community.

But almost at once there were impediments. When Jesus spoke in the synagogue of Nazareth his own people rejected him. He had come to them burning with the presence of God within, transformed by his new sense of authority and worth and they had called out from the congregation and driven him from them. The scandal of his birth was resurrected and he fled from their sneers.

Not long after, the Baptist was suddenly arrested by Herod Antipas for his condemnation of the king's marriage to his brother's widow. By his association with the Baptist, Jesus himself had suddenly become suspect, so with his small band he 'withdrew into Galilee...and went and dwelt in Capernaum by the Sea'.[2] There he would be relatively safe, for just across the water was the land of Decapolis, a group of ten self-governing cities beyond the reach of Herod's jurisdiction. Moreover, his new-found disciples had boats which could sail him to safety.

But in both cases his mission had been distorted at the very beginning by forces outside his control. Another was soon to follow. For Jesus found that despite his every effort to light the fire of repentance and rouse the people to a new and final covenant with Yahweh, they responded with demands for instant cures, for miraculous demonstrations of the healer's art, for relief from physical pain.

His anger and frustration at their selfishness, their small-minded faithlessness, overflowed again and again and, as the gospels record, he berated them roundly. Every time he effected a cure he would adjure them to keep silent about it, to attribute it to Moses or the prophets—to anyone but himself. But he could not have chosen a tactic less well suited to his ends. His reticence itself inspired them to spread the word about this modest man, so unlike the other healers with their flamboyant demonstrations and garish tricks. The lame and the leper, the blind and the epileptic flocked to him and surrounded him with their demands.

He deputised his disciples to deal with them. He retreated from the crowds to be alone. But still they sought him, still they pressed themselves upon him. It was, perhaps, the first crisis he had to confront in the purity of his self-conception. The alternatives were plain. He could reject the healing arts and devote himself solely to his teachings; or he could surrender himself to their insatiable demands.

In the end, he surrendered to them. He played the healer. He accepted that at least one of his aims had been achieved. He had attracted their attention. He had created his own forum from which to preach his message. It was a start.

It may, of course, have been that he himself believed in the efficacy of his cures, if not at first then later as the adulation of the crowds and the fawning of his disciples took effect. Also, he could rationalise that the gathering of the crowds was a sign from his Heavenly Father, an affirmation of his use of the healing so that the true message could begin to be spread.

Either way the effect upon his self-esteem was considerable. It forced upon him a new dimension of confidence and self-importance. He could see himself reflected in the eyes of his supplicants and could recall the way he had stood at the edge of the crowd as a boy and looked with reverence upon the thaumaturge and remember the longings he felt then. Now he was the centre of attention, the recipient of their devotion. That in itself was a transformation inexplicable unless the hand of God had somehow directed it.

It was a thrilling, inspirational thought and he reciprocated the love they offered him despite the selfish motives which engendered it. Their motives were unimportant. The people were about him, hanging on his words, and he was able to tell them of his vision of the world to come where the poor and the downtrodden would have their eternal revenge, where the rich and the pious and the powerful would be cast aside by God and those who, like himself, hungered for the welcoming arms of a Heavenly Father, would find their reward.

And it would be soon. If only they would repent and believe, it would be now, now before those who heard his words passed away, now before he and his disciples could even reach all the towns of Palestine to warn them of the apocalypse. All that was required was that the listeners believe. That would be the signal for Yahweh to come and for the New Kingdom to be established.

Thus armed with a growing reputation, Jesus and his Galilean disciples began their travels from Capernaum to the towns and cities of northern Palestine.[3]

There is no reason to disbelieve that he chose twelve to accompany him as his inner circle. The symbolism of the twelve tribes of Israel would not be lost on the crowds nor, more importantly, on the disciples themselves. It was one of the devices Jesus used to gain their loyalty and bind them to him, though it was certainly not the only one.

He gave them new names, symbolising the breaking of the ties with their former lives and assuaging the guilt of those who had deserted their families. It was not Simon who walked away from his wife and children but a new being who had been created—Peter, whose life found meaning only in service to Jesus.

He required them to divest themselves of their possessions, thus forcing them to become wholly dependent on him for their support.

He allowed them to break the Mosaic Law and when challenged by the Pharisees defended them against charges of desecrating the Sabbath.

By all these methods he alienated his closest followers from the broader society and through this process their dependence upon him became total.

He was not the first religious leader to use these psychological tactics on his followers but he certainly demonstrated their efficacy; the gospel accounts have become textbook models for the imposition of 'loyalty' for both religious and political organisations since. Though there are elements present in all Christian organisations, the fanatical fringe has exploited them with great enthusiasm and often to terrible effect.[4]

Another element of Jesus' mission which had the incidental effect of cementing the loyalty of his followers was his use of parables to spread his message. The stories had a multiple purpose. Some were no more than pastoral allegories; others were designed to reveal glimpses of the Kingdom of God. Still others had political overtones, the most striking being the story of the Gadarene swine. It is presented in the gospels as an incident which actually occurred to Jesus but as such it is incomprehensible.

It will be remembered that according to Mark, Jesus confronted a man 'possessed of many demons', a man driven insane by their presence within him.

Jesus calls to the demons demanding that they leave the man.

They reply, 'What have you to do with me, Jesus, son of the Most High God? I adjure you, by God, do not torment me.'

Then in a remark utterly out of character with all other dealings in demonology, Jesus asks, 'What is your name?'

Demons: 'My name is Legion, for we are many.'

The demons beg Jesus not to send them out of the country. Jesus appears to comply and instead sends them to the herd of swine feeding nearby, at which the swine rush to the sea and all are drowned.

The clue to the meaning of the parable is the identification of the demons as 'Legion'. The reference to the Legions of Rome which then 'possessed' the body politic of Israel is blindingly obvious. That Jesus was then able to cast them out of the land via the unclean swine, symbolic of Gentile filth, makes for a telling denouement, one which would have enormous appeal to his Jewish audience.

In this way, and only in this way, does the story have a point. However, because it clearly involves Jesus in the politics of his time and place the Church has declined to accept the obvious.

But with stories of this nature, the parabolic form served the purpose, as stated in Matthew, of both revealing and concealing the point. To speak openly against the Romans or their Herodian vassals was to invite the swift reprisals of arrest and imprisonment that John the Baptist had suffered. Even to hint at a messianic identity was to run a severe risk. The parable, a long respected form of teaching, was an ideal solution. Not only did it protect Jesus from the religious and political spies with their ears pricked for heresy or treason but it allowed him to favour the disciples with the real meaning behind the stories. Their sense of exclusivity was bolstered, their loyalty enhanced anew.

As they travelled through the northern cities with some disciples going ahead to rouse the people to the arrival of the Teacher, and others tending to his needs throughout the journey, the sense of achievement and of expectation within the group must have increased daily. Despite the early setbacks Jesus was beginning to make his mark. The crowds were growing, and sometimes numbered several hundred; the Pharisees and their scribes were arriving to challenge his authority, a sure sign of a growing reputation; and an increasing number of women were attaching themselves to the group, some of whom he had 'healed', others who were attracted by his fame and his charisma. Their presence, together with the funds they brought, solved some of the practical problems of the early days.

According to Mark, one day messengers arrived from John the Baptist in prison seeking the answer to a vital question: Was Jesus the Messiah? Had he been chosen and anointed by God to usher in the New Kingdom; or should they seek elsewhere for the Christ?

The passage, repeated in all its essentials in the other synoptics, utterly negates the baptismal miracle stories. For that reason, if for no other, the historicity of the event is persuasive. As such, it must have had a profound effect on Jesus.

This from John himself! That the question should be asked was itself a sign. In the silence that followed one may imagine that Jesus moved suddenly closer to his deepest longing, the belief in his kinship with the Heavenly Father. And in the presence of the adulators and supplicants the temptation to declare himself must have been great.

Yet Jesus hesitated. It is possible that he doubted the bona fides of his questioners. Already there were agents provocateurs within the crowds more than eager to report any indiscretion to their masters. Perhaps, too, there was an element of belligerence within the question. John's disciples, after all, would be hardly likely to welcome the turn of events—the former pupil outgrowing the Master.

But most likely there was still an uncertainty, an inner doubt. The magic of adoration had yet to claim him totally.

In the result, he avoided a direct answer and instead pointed to the crowds which surrounded him, the sick and the poor who came to him seeking his help. This and this alone was to be the report they should take back to John.

The caravan continued. The disciples, by now totally wedded to their master, vied with each other to serve him, flattering him unashamedly to gain his favour and spreading wildly exaggerated accounts of his deeds among the townspeople to entice them to his meetings.

Then came the shattering news of John's death: beheaded in the court of Herod Antipas to satisfy the vengeance of his new wife, the adulteress Herodias, against whom he had spoken.

The effect upon Jesus must have been swift and profound. At first there would be the human pain of loss. The man who had been so close to him, who had inspired him to begin his ministry, who had seen in him the possibility of Divine Anointing, had been snatched away at the whim of a harlot!

Then would come the fear for himself and his company. If Herod was capable of this act, no one was safe, least of all the known associates of the Baptist.

But on reflection, had it not been John who had proclaimed himself the herald of the one who was to come, the true Messiah who would lead the elect of Israel like a new Moses to the Promised Land? Could not this terrible news be interpreted as a sign from Yahweh that the time had come for the Messiah to declare himself? Perhaps the Father had decided that John's work was done and He had gathered him to Him. In so doing, perhaps He was giving a signal to all His people that at last the time was ripe for the emergence of the Anointed One.

Still Jesus hesitated. As was his custom, he withdrew to pray alone and to listen to the urgings of his need and to find there the voice of a Heavenly Father.

Soon afterwards, we may believe, one of the leading ladies of Herod's court, Joanna, the wife of his steward, arrived to join the company. Most likely she was the source of further disturbing news—that the King was aware of his activities and fearful that the soul of John had entered Jesus and was returning to plague him.

It was another fear, another factor to add to all the rest in deciding what must be done next. It must have been an overwhelming decision to confront, at times the choice so clear, the knowledge so certain, and at others the terrible self-doubts joining with the fear of its consequences to damn the idea utterly.

It may well have been at this point that Jesus decided to put the decision to the test, to send out the disciples 'two by two' to the people of the surrounding villages and towns to proclaim the coming of the Messiah and to gauge their reaction. If the people rose en masse to affirm their belief the movement would gather an impetus which would sweep through the land and he would be venerated, not as a healer but as the true Messiah, the earthly symbol of Yahweh, the leader of the Elect.

And while they were proclaiming the news in the north, Jesus himself with his young favourite, Judas, would head south to Jerusalem and listen to the words of his small band of followers there and the answer would become clear.

If nothing else, the temporary disbanding of the group would foil any plans Herod might have for their capture.

But whether in fact Jesus made the journey to Jerusalem or not, the report from his Galilean disciples when he was reunited with them was devastating. Demons had been cast out, they said, the sick had been anointed with oil, but there it ended. The people had not believed, they had not flocked to them to be led back to the Master; they had not begun the brushfire of faith which would blaze through the land and consume the opposition. The people, as usual, had sought cures for their bodily ills. That was what they cared about. It was all they cared about, all they cared about...

Perhaps it was then, as Matthew indicates, that Jesus flew into a monumental rage and cried out against the people of the cities:

'Woe to you, Chorazin! Woe to you, Bethsaida! For if the mighty works done in you had been done in Tyre and Sidon they would have repented long ago in sackcloth and ashes. But I tell you, it shall be more tolerable for Tyre and Sidon on the day of judgement than for you. And you, Capernaum, will you be exalted to heaven? You shall be brought down to Hades! For if the mighty works done in you had been done in Sodom, it would have remained until this day. But I tell you it shall be more tolerable on the day of judgement for the land of Sodom than for you!'[5]

It is a remarkable passage and it reveals a man consumed with savagery and totally out of control, damning whole populations—rich and poor, weak and powerful—to eternal hellfire. They are the words, not of a peaceful teacher of righteousness, but of a deeply vulnerable human being who has been rejected and has allowed the streak of cruelty which inhabits all such men to pour forth in a tirade.

Almost certainly it is not a single outburst but, as with so many of the speeches attributed to Jesus, the distillation of an attitude which lasted for days or even weeks. And it would not be surprising in a man whose analogies ran so often to the supping of wine that in this period Jesus himself sought consolation in the red liquor of oblivion. Indeed, the passage itself reads suspiciously like the drunken maunderings of a small man in pain.

Perhaps it was then that the hated Pharisees came to taunt him with his overindulgence and received from him the bitter reply:

'For John came neither eating nor drinking and they say, "He has a demon"; the Son of Man came eating and drinking and they say, "Behold a glutton and a drunkard, a friend of tax collectors and sinners".'6

But the Pharisees were not easily put off and it is clear that they had found an effective counter to the high-flown claims being put about by the disciples. Even his healing was suspect, they said. If in fact he healed—a doubtful proposition at best—he did so at the behest of Beelzebub, the arch demon himself, the prince of drunkards. It was a tag which would remain with Jesus throughout his ministry.

But from within that terrible period of depression and failure came the decision which would guide the course of his ministry from then until his death. It was clear at last that the people as a whole would never make the act of obeisance to Yahweh, the declaration of repentance necessary for the will of God to be fulfilled and for the New Kingdom to be inaugurated. Equally, it was plain that not even the devotion of a group of men—the elect of the Elect—was sufficient to bring about the divine intervention. No, the responsibility finally and forever devolved upon one man.

And that man was the Messiah.

Of course, it cannot be known with certainty when the full realisation of Jesus' messianic identity forced itself upon him. The gospel evidence is contradictory; scholars are divided. Many take the view that from the moment of the baptism his messianic identity was utterly clear to him and that he acted throughout in response to its demands.

But if that is the case, the 'Great Confession' at Caesarea Philippi, long after the ministry had begun, makes no sense at all. For it is here that Jesus draws his disciples into discussion with the words: 'Who do men say that I am?'7 The disciples, one may imagine, are taken aback. They reply that some believe he is John the Baptist reincarnate; others that he is Elijah, again reincarnate; still others that he is simply one of the prophets risen to life. Their replies are delivered without the slightest editorial comment. They appear as simply the response to one seeking information.

Then he says: 'But who do you say that I am?'

Again, the response is significant. Had he declared himself to be the Messiah prior to this time the question would have no point at all. Indeed, had he even hinted at his messianic identity among those so eager to flatter him and proclaim his prowess, the asking of the question would, at best, have been merely a demand for a chorus of affirmation.

But instead all are silent but Peter. Into the silence, Peter says, 'You are the Christ.'

Then, according to Mark, 'he charged them to tell no one about him'.

It is quite clearly, the first time the question has been asked of the disciples, though it may well have been that they themselves had hinted at it to the Galilean populace in their attempts to raise the multitudes. For Jesus, however, it is indeed the Great Confession, the first occasion in all his life that he is able to articulate the thought which had been burning inside him.

It occurs in the synoptics after the failure of the disciples' mission, though it is quite impossible to reach any firm conclusion from the gospels on the timing or even the order of the events they describe. But the passage has all the earmarks of a finale to a drama through which all the participants have lived: of great expectations followed by crushing failure; of the Master's raging and railing against the faithless generation who cannot or will not accept the truth and the significance of his message; and of violent and uncontrolled scenes as Jesus worked out the anger and the frustration from his being. This was followed by his withdrawal from his closest associates into that world of the spirit where none could reach him, of speculation among them as the days passed and still he kept to himself and no one dared approach. Then finally one evening as they sat in their camp by the roadside or gathered in the square of a village his presence was suddenly among them, a new gravity in his bearing, a sense of exultation restrained only by the fearful consequences of his decision.

Then the questions: surprising questions. They knew him to be Yesu'a, the Master. Was that not enough? Clearly he sought more from them. He wanted them to say the word which had often passed between them though never in his presence, the word which encapsulated the great dream of Israel within its syllables but which men spoke only in whispers. He would not say it himself. It must come from them. He led them to it and waited. Finally, Peter allowed it to escape his lips: 'Messiah.'

He nodded his agreement. When he told them to tell no one about him, they instantly agreed.

In Matthew's rendering of the occasion a small passage has been added, one which has had enormous consequences for mankind. When Peter identifies him as the Christ, Jesus is overwhelmed. 'Blessed are you, Simon Bar-Jonah! For flesh and blood has not revealed this to you but my Father who is in heaven. And I tell you, you are Peter and on this rock I will build my church, and the power of death shall not prevail against it. I will give you the keys of the Kingdom of Heaven and whatever you bind on earth shall be bound in Heaven and whatever you loose on earth shall be loosed in Heaven.'[8]

The Roman Catholic Church claiming direct descent from Peter relies on this passage for its authority. This, despite the fact that all the other gospels contradict it outright [Peter having received his sect name long before the incident] and in Matthew the passage is followed by a vicious denunciation of Peter by

Jesus himself: 'Get behind me, Satan! You are a hindrance to me, for you are not on the side of God but of men.'⁹

The passage is obviously a much later interpolation but no doubt Catholic scholars see it differently. To accept the obvious is to reveal the authority of the Pope and his Church as a silly fiction.

According to all the synoptics, Jesus then began to tell the disciples that the Son of Man 'must suffer many things and be treated with contempt'.

There is no way of knowing precisely the sources of Jesus' vision of the manner in which the Messiah must fulfil his mission so as to be assured that it met the requirements of his Heavenly Father. But we may be certain that there was, in fact, a plan. It would be quite inconceivable for anyone to embark on what was to be, quite literally, an apocalyptic mission without some foreknowledge of the manner in which it was to be conducted.

Some would argue that he could have received this knowledge as a revelation in prayer, but there is certainly no indication of this in the narratives. Even if it were so, the strong probability is that Jesus would have sought confirmation by reference to the holy words of Yahweh as revealed to the prophets.

In this respect there is a passage which so parallels the actual course of events as described by the synoptics that it is impossible to ignore it. It is from the Old Testament book of Isaiah written by the later of the two authors of the book and known by scholars as Deutero-Isaiah, with which Jesus was well acquainted.[10]

It is a passage which must have struck deep into the heart of Jesus. In fact, it may have seemed to have been written with no other purpose than to guide him to a destiny prepared by God. It is the story of the Suffering Servant of the Lord.

According to Isaiah, whose words were much discussed by the Essenes, such a man 'had no form or comeliness that we should look at him and no beauty that we should desire him'.

He was despised and rejected by men; a man of sorrows, and acquainted with grief; and as one from whom men hid their faces he was despised and we esteemed him not.

Thus identified, it would have seemed to Jesus that the rest spoke only to him. It is a long passage but it bears quoting at length.

Surely he has borne our griefs and carried our sorrows; yet we esteemed him stricken, smitten by God and afflicted. But he was wounded for our transgressions; he was bruised for our iniquities; upon him was the chastisement that made us whole, and with his stripes we are healed.

All we, like sheep, have gone astray; we have turned everyone to his own way; and the Lord has laid on him the iniquity of us all.

He was oppressed and he was afflicted, yet he opened not his mouth; like a lamb that is led to the slaughter, and like a sheep that before its shearers is dumb, so he opened not his mouth.

By oppression and judgement he was taken away; and as for his generation, who considered that he was cut off out of the land of the living, stricken for the transgression of my people? And they made his grave with the wicked and with a rich man in his death, although he had done no violence, and there was no deceit in his mouth.

Yet it was the will of the Lord to bruise him; he has put him to grief; when he makes himself an offering for sin, he shall see his offspring, he shall prolong his days; the will of the Lord shall prosper in his hand; he shall see the fruit of the travail of his soul and be satisfied; by his knowledge that the righteous one, my servant, make many to be accounted righteous; and he shall bear their iniquities.

Therefore I will divide him a portion with the great, and he shall divide the spoil with the strong; because he poured out his soul to death, and was numbered with the transgressors; yet he bore the sin of many and made intercession for the transgressors.[11]

There is no way of knowing, of course, whether the passage commended itself to Jesus at the time, though there can be no doubt that he was aware of it. Nor is there any suggestion that these were the only writings from Biblical works which were favoured by the Essenes that Jesus relied upon to guide him through the rest of his public life. But at the risk of prophesying after the event, the parallels between the ancient scenario and the facts of Jesus' activity as portrayed by the synoptics are so striking that it would be more remarkable if he had not been affected by them.

In orthodox Christian teaching the importance of this great decision on Jesus' part has been either ignored or deliberately underplayed. It has not suited the theological deifiers to admit to their dogma the deeply human emotion surrounding it. They would have it that the deified Son of God was simply fulfilling an immutable plan predestined from the very moment of creation. Within that framework Jesus can be seen as no more than a puppet dancing to the will of God. Others, while admitting the existence of his capacity for choice—in varying degrees—have concentrated on the pain of crucifixion as evidence of his physical courage. But even in this they have centred their opinion on a belief that he was, after all, superhuman and totally aware of the outcome of his act: the resurrection which would inevitably follow.

Thus, the true significance of his decision has been lost. In this sense it matters little that the vision of his destiny was dredged from the depths of his despair at the rejection from his own kind, wrought from pain, and based on a terrible delusion.

Even the facts of his background, the great chasms of need which drove him to the brink of madness in a frantic search for completeness, are less important than the decision he took and which he revealed at Caesarea Philippi. For whatever the forces which drove him to it and however mistaken it proved to be, his courage and strength of will is revealed in the determination he showed in the months to follow when he pursued it to the end.

Notes

1. Mark 1:14.
2. Matthew 4:12.
3. According to Mark they would journey together to Gennesaret, Tyre and Sidon, the Decapolis region and the district of Dalmanutha before reaching Caesarea Philippi and then turning their steps toward Jerusalem.
4. The methods of Charles Manson and Jim Jones, leader of the infamous Guyana mass suicide, owed much to the principles which Jesus exploited. However, it must be said that beside the bloodshed which has accompanied the promulgation of the Christian faith the activities of Manson and Jones are quite insignificant.
5. Matthew 11:21-24.
6. Matthew 11:18-19.
7. Mark 8:27-38.
8. Matthew 16:17-20.
9. Matthew 16:23.
10. See Luke 4:17; Matthew 8:17-20. Significantly, Isaiah was a ritual element in the teachings of the Essenes and is contained in the scrolls discovered at Qumran.
11. Isaiah 53:3-12.

12

The Messiah

¹FROM the moment of the declaration of his messianic identity to the disciples a new element enters Jesus' life, a sense of purpose and of strength which has hitherto come only in fits and starts. Now there is a clear road ahead and it leads, inevitably, to Jerusalem.

It is almost as though he has been able to look back upon his life and see it as a preparation for the great decision, as though the deepest longings cherished through adolescence and young manhood have at last been fulfilled. Henceforth he is able to see himself as the loving and dutiful Son of God working the will of his Heavenly Father.

There is also a none-too-subtle change in Jesus' relations with his disciples: where once he was forced to chastise them for the inconstancy of their belief, now his chief concern seems to be in arbitrating their squabbles over the spoils of the New Kingdom on earth.

His vision of the New Kingdom is now clear. At its centre is a Day of Judgement; on that day the world will be transformed and the 'righteous' men of Judaism will become the spiritual arbiters of all humanity.

The Gentiles will be cast aside and from among his disciples twelve judges will decide on the future of all men and women now living. The sheep will be separated from the goats. The fortunate—the poor, the downcast—will be granted eternal bliss in the presence of Yahweh. The rest—from the arrogant

Sadducees to the Roman oppressors—will be cast into hell where for all time they will 'weep and gnash their teeth'.

And he, Yesu'a, will sit on the right hand of Power, overseeing the apocalypse. The Suffering Servant will have unlocked the key to a new and glorious existence.[2]

After the disciples' return to the house they had established in Capernaum, Jesus questions them:

'What were you discussing on the way?' But they were silent; for on the way they had discussed with one another who was the greatest. And he sat down and called the twelve; and he said to them, 'If any one would be first, he must be last of all and servant of all.'[3]

It is an attitude fully in keeping with the vision of the Suffering Servant. However, among the disciples there are no applicants for the position. Instead, they change the subject at the first opportunity.

A little later, James and John Boanerges try a more direct approach. They ask quite openly to be given pride of place in the New Kingdom on his left and right hand. Jesus replies diplomatically that the choice is not really his to make but the prerogative of his Heavenly Father.

In Matthew, the disciples enlist their mother to plead on their behalf but with the same result. The accounts are by no means mutually exclusive.

But beneath the bickering within the company it is clear that Jesus himself has a much deeper concern. It is with the act of suffering which he must undergo in order to bring about the final intervention of his Heavenly Father in the affairs of men. It is not by any means a preoccupation with the physical pain involved. Rather it is an obsessive need to fulfil the requirements of Yahweh to the last particular.

In this respect, much has been made of the three passages in Mark in which Jesus predicts his death and subsequent resurrection three days later. While it seems likely that in revealing his vision of himself as the Messiah Jesus went on to speak of the suffering he would have to ensure, the so-called predictions have all the appearance of editorial additions long after the apostles had claimed a resurrection and raised it to an article of faith.

In Mark, for example, the account in which Jesus charges the disciples to reveal his identity to no man suddenly changes from a direct quotation to an indirect report: 'And he began to teach them that the Son of Man must suffer many things, and be rejected by the elders and the chief priests and the scribes, and be killed, and after three days rise again'. Then, as though to validate the claim—in the manner of all self-conscious elaborators—the evangelist (or the editor) feels obliged to add, 'And he said this plainly'.

The particularity of the report is suspicious, as is the change in style, but then comes a remarkable passage. Mark says: 'And Peter took him, and began to rebuke him. But turning to his disciples he rebuked Peter, and said, "Get behind me, Satan! For you are not on the side of God but of men."' Then, as if incensed, Jesus calls a 'multitude' to him and says, incomprehensibly:

> 'If any man would come after me (the Messiah!) let him deny himself and take up his cross and follow me. For whoever would save his life would lose it; and whoever loses his life for my sake and for the gospel will save it. For what does it profit a man to gain the whole world and forfeit his life? For what can a man give in return for his life? For whoever is ashamed of me and of my words in this adulterous and sinful generation, of him will the Son of Man also be ashamed, when he comes in the glory of his father with the holy angels.'[4]

Thus the gospel would have it that immediately after Jesus warned his disciples to tell no man of his identity he himself broke the news to a 'multitude'.

It may well have been that in the emotion of the announcement from Jesus concerning his suffering that Peter protested and Jesus rebuked him. But the sudden arrival of the multitude conjured up from nowhere and Jesus' exhortation in such unlikely terms—'for whoever is ashamed of me...of him the Son of Man will also be ashamed'—it is quite clearly a later addition. There is no suggestion from the disciples that anyone is 'ashamed' of Jesus, and certainly not the all-purpose multitude. No one had raised the question of shame at that stage. That was all in the future when the embattled Christians were being howled to scorn over their claims of resurrection and messiahship for their departed leader. Only in that context does the passage make any sense whatever. The three 'predictions' are in the same category—the work of editors and apologists.

Interestingly, Jesus' speech overflows into a single verse in the following chapter: 'And he said to them (the multitude) "Truly, I say to you, there are some standing here who will not taste death before they see the Kingdom of God come with power"'[5] Unlike the foregoing, this saying captures perfectly the essence of his message following the great decision. His time, and consequently that of the New Kingdom, has almost come.

It also indicates that this was a period of growing excitement within the group. By whatever route, they were heading inevitably to Jerusalem and to the self-induced climax of the drama. The disciples were naturally on edge, exhilarated at the prospect of the transformation of the world and their place as judges in the New Kingdom, yet fearful of the crisis which must precede it. For it was clear from his analogies and his bearing that the Master was planning some act of atonement and they would inevitably become involved, whatever it was.

Jesus himself would have more and more frequently felt the need to escape from their society to commune with himself in prayer, bolstering his will to continue. On one such occasion, it seems, a small group of disciples followed him and on their return claimed to have seen him transfigured, 'his garments glistening, intensely white, as no fuller on earth could bleach them'. In the retelling they claimed to have seen not only the prophet Elijah but Moses himself in conversation with Jesus. More yet, for once again there was the 'Divine megaphone' of the baptism proclaiming: 'This is my beloved Son; listen to him'.[6]

The story is quite in keeping with the sense of mild hysteria which would affect any group on such a mission. It increases in intensity the closer they come to the capital. At the side of the road a blind man is pictured crying out, 'Jesus, Son of David, have mercy on me!'

The company rebukes him and tells him to be silent. Apparently, by now Jesus has eschewed the healing arts. But the blind man multiplies his cries and Jesus is forced to relent. He cures the man who, according to Mark, immediately joins the company.[7]

The passage is doubly significant in revealing the new sense of authority in Jesus, since the blind man's cry ('Son of David') was a title reserved for the Messiah and on this occasion Jesus makes no attempt to contradict him.

Onward they travel towards Jerusalem: Jesus and his disciples, the wealthy women who provided for them and the poor who tended their needs. Perhaps others sought their company, forerunners of the pilgrims coming from Galilee to celebrate the Passover in the holy city, unaware that the Teacher in the midst of his adoring flock was about to proclaim himself the long-awaited Messiah. In so doing, he would keep alive the fire of resistance to Roman oppression which would blaze forth thirty years later to consume their loved ones in the great war.

But to Jesus and his inner circle such a future would have been inconceivable. For the Kingdom of God would be established not in thirty years, not even in thirty days, but at the height of the celebrations to which all were travelling: and when that occurred war would end forever. In its place a world of 'righteousness' would prevail and the nations of the earth would be as supplicants to the chosen nation of God, the Elect of Israel, and sitting on the right hand of God interceding for all would be Yesu'a, 'The Help of Yahweh', despised and rejected by men but beloved of his heavenly Father.

In addition to the scriptural requirements—the fulfilment of prophecy which Jesus must accomplish in his role of Messiah—it was necessary for him to understand the temporal forces at work in Jerusalem and to bend them to his will to achieve his aims. It required no great political expertise on Jesus' part to understand the volatile situation into which he was deliberately injecting himself. As we have seen, the probability is that he had been in Jerusalem himself fairly recently or at least had first-hand information from his trusted Judas. But even without such intelligence he, like any one from Palestine, would have learned of the outrage committed by the Procurator, Pontius Pilate, who had commandeered sacred Temple funds to build a new viaduct into the city.

Like all good Jews, Jesus would have been shocked and angry at the Roman's effrontery in laying hands on the treasury. However, the keenness of his anger would not have been as great as that of the Sadducees and in particular the aristocratic, priestly family of Annas, whose son-in-law Caiaphas was presently Chief Priest. They seem to have regarded the treasure—the source of their wealth and power—as a personal trust.

Annas and his group were the most powerful bloc in the Sanhedrin, the supreme ecclesiastical council of Israel, and that body was now locked in a power struggle with the Procurator. So intense and vicious was the struggle that within a year their excesses would cause Caiaphas to be deposed and Pilate to be recalled to Rome to answer charges of cruelty, corruption and tyranny.[8]

The Sanhedrin believed that if they could demonstrate to the Roman Emperor Tiberius that Pilate was being unnecessarily provocative and that the Jewish people could be trusted with a greater measure of self-determination within the Empire, then they would be given a freer hand to run the nation's affairs. For his part, Pilate wanted no more than any of his predecessors throughout the Empire: to be allowed to amass a huge personal fortune by graft and corruption before returning to the civilised company of Rome with honour and a measure of glory.

By the time Jesus was ready to make his triumphal entrance to the city the Sanhedrin had gained a distinct advantage. Pilate had learned well the methods of the Zealots and had suppressed a protest against his use of the Temple treasure by dressing his soldiers in civilian clothes to mingle with the protestors. Then, on signal, they threw off their cloaks and cut loose with knife and sword from within the crowd.

The Sanhedrin could not have asked for better if they had organised the blood-letting themselves. The common people might not have been as outraged as they over the use of the treasure—after all, the money was used to provide them with much-needed water supplies—but this cowardly slaughter of their brethren must surely have rekindled all the old hatreds. So, with the people demonstrably allied to them, if only in common hatred of the Procurator, the Jewish leaders were in a position of strength.

The one contingency they had to guard against was the very one which even now was advancing on the city—an unruly band of illiterate Galileans fervent with excitement at the prospect of their leader, a typical deluded 'miracle worker' declaring himself the Messiah at the very doors of the Temple.

If that were allowed to occur, the Sanhedrin's advantage would almost certainly be lost. As their spies had reported, the man was an effective rabble-rouser. Already his reputation as a healer had preceded him and that would be enough to assure him of substantial crowds. There was even a report that he had raised one Lazarus from the dead! Clearly, the 'dead' man was a confederate who had joined with the fellow to perpetrate the 'miracle', but the people were as gullible as ever and who could tell what might happen if he were given free rein.

And at such a time! The year A.D. 36 was a taxation year when the people felt, as they did every fourteen years, the full weight of their burden as vassals of Rome. Given half a chance they would react as they had so often before: in futile rebellion against the power of the Empire. If that were to occur suddenly it would be Pilate, and not they, who would point the accusing finger. He would laugh to scorn their claims for peaceful self-determination within the Empire.

Such a thought was intolerable. Whatever the cost, it simply must not be allowed to eventuate. The man must be dealt with…for the good of Israel.

Whether through his own visit or reports from the Beloved Disciple or the favourite Judas with his Zealot connections, there can be little doubt that Jesus was aware of the delicate situation which prevailed in the city. In no sense was this a hindrance to his plan. On the contrary, it meant that it was open for him to manipulate the contending forces to his own ends. And on the evidence of his words and actions, he did so with considerable skill.

According to the fourth gospel, the Annas group had taken the decision well before his arrival that 'one man should die for the people that the whole nation should not perish'.[9] This was not the sort of intelligence which could remain secret for long and if, as seems likely, the Beloved Disciple was a Temple Priest he would be in an excellent position to hear of it and to transmit it to Jesus.

One can only imagine the effect the news must have had on Jesus. From this distance and with the available evidence it is not possible to know precisely the details of his plan for the realisation of his act of atonement. Much of it can only be conjectured. All that is certain is that it would end with his offering himself for crucifixion.

In that sense the news would not have been unwelcome. Even before his arrival in the capital the concluding act in the drama had been secured. But before that could be allowed to occur there were important conditions to be met. Proclamations must be made both by word and deed. Prophecies must be fulfilled. Men must be given the opportunity to see him and to believe in him before the final hour. And, most importantly, the conclusion must arrive at his behest. All the circumstances of his suffering must remain under his control; nothing must be allowed to interfere with the divine plan he was following.

Some little time before the Passover he arrived at Bethany, a town on the outskirts of the capital, and there he stayed with Martha and Mary. The house was well situated for his purposes. Its distance from Jerusalem—about ten kilometres—meant a strenuous regimen for himself and the disciples who had to walk there and back each day of the following week. But that was itself an excellent protection from a surprise raid by agents of the Sanhedrin or by soldiers from the garrison of Antonia.

From his vantage point he could organise his followers in Jerusalem and in this respect there was much to be done. He could also keep in touch with the main body of Galilean pilgrims who were due to arrive and at whose head he would ride in triumph into the city.

Moreover, it was a congenial headquarters for him. Martha and Mary were devoted to him and all the gospels carry stories of their attentions. It was a home where he was offered a measure of peach and of love and though the sisters were jealous of each other that, too, would be balm to the soul of one who had craved affection for so long.

But even as he rested his body prior to the arrival of the Galileans the knowledge and the fear of that ordeal would never have been far from his mind. The sheer magnitude of the task demanded his complete attention. Even if he had wanted to share his burden, there was no one he was able to trust with the entirety of his plan. If those who loved him learned of his intentions they would surely try to dissuade him; however well-meaning their motives, the risk was too great, the odds too high.

Each had his own part to play—the Galilean disciples to stir up the crowds on his behalf and to act as his immediate bodyguard; the Judeans to keep him informed of the Sanhedrin's plans and to undertake specific tasks which would allow him to fulfil the prophecies; and Judas, his young intimate, who had the most demanding role of all.

Each had to be dealt with; each had to know and appreciate the importance of his allotted duty. And when that was done there was the need, as ever, to commune in prayer and to feel once more the power beneath his prayer, the guiding hand of his need, the Heavenly Father.

So when his messenger came running to report the arrival of the Galilean pilgrims one may believe that a new urgency, bordering on ecstasy, propelled him as he led his disciples forward and joined the boisterous crowd. The first step in his planning was about to be realised.

As they travelled towards the city he called two of his followers to him and told them, 'Go into the village opposite you, and immediately as you enter it you will find a colt tied, on which no one has ever sat; untie it and bring it. If anyone says to you, "Why are you doing this?" say, "The Lord has need of it and will send it back here immediately."'

The disciples ran and did as they were bid. The colt was waiting just as Jesus had planned. The Judean disciple had not failed him. His followers returned with it and Jesus mounted the animal and urged it forward to the centre of the procession.

The gates of Jerusalem loomed ahead. The rest of the Galilean disciples were deployed through the crowd, prepared to begin the great shout of triumph as he entered. The colt was steady beneath him; the gates yawned open. At last it was beginning and it was happening as he had willed it, for was it not written by the great Zechariah, "Fear not, daughter of Zion; behold your king is coming...sitting on an ass' colt!'?[10]

From somewhere within the crowd the first cry was heard. 'Hosanna! Blessed is he who comes in the name of the Lord...Hosanna in the highest!' Momentarily, others followed, palm branches were torn from the trees and strewn before him; he passed through the shadow of the portico and from all sides the glorious cry echoed through the narrow streets to the small, misshapen man on the donkey: 'Hosanna! Blessed is he who comes in the name of the Lord.'[11]

The Messiah had declared himself to the world.

Notes

1. Mark 11:1-4.
2. Mark 12:38-40, 13:24-27, 14:62; Matthew 11:20-24, 18:8, 19:24-30; Luke 13:1-3, 23-30, 17:24-30; John 5:24-30.

3. Mark 9:34-35.
4. Mark 8:34-38.
5. Mark 9:1.
6. Mark 9:3-7; 1:10-11.
7. Mark 10:47-52.
8. Little is known of Pontius Pilate's early life. He enters history (via Josephus) only when he is appointed Procurator of Judea in A.D. 27. His patron was the anti-Semitic Sejanus, favourite of the Emperor Tiberius, but unfortunately for Pilate Sejanus was unable to secure a like-minded appointee as Governor of Syria, his immediate superior. The Jews sought to exploit the weakness of Pilate's position, particularly after the fall of Sejanus in A.D. 31. Pilate, it seems, became increasingly hostile and perhaps even unstable. His provocative attack on the Samaritans in A.D. 36-37 caused his recall to Rome and according to Eusebius he committed suicide, probably as an alternative to being publicly disgraced by the Senate. His wife, Claudia, is said to have been distantly related to the Imperial family. Caiaphas, too, was deposed by the Governor of Syria (Vitellius) for his hand in the Samaritan massacre (Josephus, Antiquities).
9. John 11:49-51.
10. Matthew 21:5.
11. Matthew 21:9-10.

13

Jerusalem!

NEWS of the Nazarene's spirited entry to the capital quickly spread through the crowded city and with each retelling became the more audacious and incredible. He had allowed himself to be called the Messiah! Some said he welcomed it. There was even a report that when a group of Pharisees demanded that he should silence his followers Jesus retorted, 'I tell you, if these were silent the very stones would cry out!'[1]

Obviously, the man was a fool. The Sanhedrin would be incensed. They would have to act against him. They must.

But however misguided the man might be there was no doubting his courage. And he was the one, some said, who had performed the miraculous cures—restoring a blind man's sight, giving a paralytic the power to walk, even raising a man from the dead!

But was he not also the one the Pharisees said scorned the Sabbath rules, ate and drank himself stupid, associated with harlots and tax collectors and even an adulteress from the court of Herod Antipas? And a Nazarene at that! For was it not said by all that nothing good ever came out of Nazareth? Heaven forbid that such a man should come as the Anointed One.

And yet...was it not also said by John the Baptist that another would follow him who would be the anointed of God, and was not this Yesu'a a member of John's company? Perhaps the soul of John had entered him and he had returned in this clever, secret guise to bring forth the Last of the Days and to usher in the New Kingdom. Was it not possible?

After all, how far could the Pharisees be trusted in these matters? They had refused to accept John as a true prophet. They had hardly raised a whimper when Herod had put him to death for a crime that was no crime at all. Instead they had stood cravenly by while the harlot Herodias flaunted her marital blasphemy before the world and John had paid the penalty for speaking the truth.

Perhaps there was something to this man. Even if he were not the Messiah, perhaps he was a prophet, one who would take the place of John and become a standard-bearer for the people's hopes, a spiritual conscience unafraid to rebuke the lordly and the blasphemous even unto death. Perhaps. Certainly his presence in the city would make for a lively Passover.

The ruling faction of the Sanhedrin can have entertained no similar sense of pleasurable expectancy. By the manner of his entry to the city Jesus had, in one sense, played into their hands. The waverers on the council, the liberals, would close ranks behind them. No longer would there be any doubt about the Nazarene's intentions. Like Judas the Galilean thirty years ago, he was a troublemaker prepared to go to any lengths to stir the people to his cause, even to the point of having himself declared the Messiah. Now they would see him as the Annas faction did: as an ignorant, backwoods fool who did not understand the importance of what the Sanhedrin was trying to do, or how much he was acting against the real interests of the people.

But, it had to be admitted that in choosing that particular method of declaring himself he had caused more problems than anticipated. Had he come unannounced and in secret as he had in the past, it would have been simple to track him down and quietly put him away until the celebrations were over. Then they could bring him to justice at a time and place of their own choosing.

Even if he had simply arrived with his company of rowdies and female camp followers the situation could have been handled with a minimum of fuss. Pilate could have been induced to round them up with a handful of soldiers and hardly anyone would have been aware of it since the vast majority of pilgrims in the city had never heard of him and the natives cared little for Galilean fanatics.

But now there was an entirely different problem confronting them. By the very act of declaring himself the Messiah he had set the whole city talking and anything they did now would be done in the spotlight of public attention.

Their course, then, was clear. They must confront him in public and discredit him before the crowds. They must force him to condemn himself from his own mouth. Once that was achieved—and surely it could be accomplished with a modicum of effort; he was, after all, merely a northern rabble-rouser—the way would be clear for them to remove him without themselves rousing the populace to anger.

It takes little imagination to envisage a hastily assembled group of Sadducees, Pharisees and scribes bent to the task of constructing questions which would be put to him whenever the crowds surrounded him. On the evidence of the gospels, this is precisely what happened.

According to Mark, the three questions they settled on were beautifully crafted for their purposes. Each demanded a response which would damn him irrevocably.

They would challenge him to declare openly—with his own words this time, not by some stage-managed demonstration—the authority by which he preached. If he did believe himself to be the Messiah, let him say it aloud. When and if he did, they would then have the opportunity for a demonstration of their own, this time against the blasphemer, the Galilean upstart. And with the shocked and pious crowd behind them he would be removed in a single stroke.

If he escaped the first question, another would be in readiness. Since everyone was complaining about the hated poll tax they would ask his opinion on whether it should be paid. If he answered yes, he would immediately lose favour with the people; but if no, then he was obviously guilty of treason to the Emperor and Pilate's soldiers would be forced to arrest him as an agitator.

And if he survived those they would have yet another: a question on the very subject which had sent John to the Herodian sword—divorce. Everyone would be immediately aware of its implications. If he approved the marriage between Herod Antipas and his harlot wife he would be denying John and the people would justly hold him in contempt. But if he repeated John's admonition he would be guilty of John's crime and would, therefore, be seized by Herod's bodyguard who had travelled to the capital with their king for the Passover. His fate would be the same as John's.

Thus armed, it must have seemed to the Annas faction and their collaborators on the Sanhedrin that the Yesu'a problem was already solved. The 'scenario' was watertight.

The unfolding of the drama of the final week of Jesus' life is difficult to reconstruct in detail since in this phase the chronologies of the synoptics and the fourth gospel are directly contradictory. Also, it is obvious that there have been considerable elaborations and interpolations not only in Matthew and Luke (as would be expected) but to a lesser extent in Mark as well.

All the gospels record lengthy sermonising by Jesus, as though the authors are aware that the story has not long to run and are anxious to make their various points before the close.

The synoptics introduce a number of inappropriate parables and the incomprehensible story of a fig tree which Jesus is said to have withered in a fit of pique. Matthew and Luke take the opportunity to spew virulence at 'the Jews' through Jesus' mouth in the wilful abasement of humanity which religion alone appears able to inspire.

Nevertheless, the principal elements of the confrontation batter their way through the prejudices and the interpolations so that even from the distance of twenty centuries the essentials are clear.

Once the triumphal entry had been achieved the die was cast. Now it was move and countermove: the Sanhedrin attempting to have Jesus condemn himself from his own mouth; and Jesus fighting to maintain intact all the elements of the plan he had conceived as being divinely written, a plan which had to be followed to the last detail if he were to prepare the way for the apocalypse. But in this Jesus had a singular advantage. The Sanhedrin could not know that the contending sides were in fact working toward the same end: the voluntary sacrifice of the Suffering Servant. They could not know, for he had told no one more than was necessary for each to complete his part successfully. They could not know because no rational man would expect that another was plotting his own crucifixion, and certainly not the religious politicians of the Sanhedrin who had grown fat in the service of Yahweh.

It cannot be known whether the reverse applied and that Jesus was ignorant of the countermoves plotted by the Sanhedrin clique. However, religious politicians are no different from the secular variety in their propensity to talk of their momentous decisions to friends and associates they wish to impress. In the even, Jesus seems to have been well prepared for the three fateful questions when they did arise. It may have been that once again the Beloved Disciple proved his worth. But the point is not an important one. The sharpness of Jesus' mind is not questioned, particularly at this period of heightened awareness in the shadow of the cross. However disturbed his emotional state, his actions alone in marshalling his meagre forces against the combined might of the Sanhedrin, the Romans and Herod Antipas, bear eloquent testimony to the acuteness of his intelligence. Indeed, this is perfectly illustrated in the next dramatic step in the confrontation, for it is Jesus who once again seizes the initiative.

In staging the messianic entry to the capital he had thrown down the gauntlet to the Sanhedrin and, in effect, publicly introduced himself to the masses gathered there. But according to Mark and Matthew (and not contradicted by Luke or John) once the entry had been accomplished he returned immediately to Bethany. This was not only a prudent move to avoid his enemies in the city, but it suited perfectly his plans for the following day.

It permitted the single declarative act to stand alone and for news of it to spread through the populace so that when he returned eyes would follow his progress; a crowd would gather about him if only to see what would happen next. Their presence would afford him the best protection of all. With a volatile multitude about him none of the authorities would dare try to take him by force.

But much more was needed from the crowd than simple curiosity. He had to gain their attention for a much deeper reason. He had to reach them with his message—that the Kingdom of God was at hand. He had to call upon them to repent and believe. And by his actions, as well as his words, he had to reveal to them the nature of the Kingdom, the essence of the new covenant.

The method he chose was little short of masterly. With his disciples surrounding him and a multitude following in his wake he advanced on the outer court of the Temple. Here the moneychangers plied their trade, exchanging Roman and other foreign coinage for the Jewish currency which alone was acceptable as a Temple offering. This was necessary since invariably the foreign coins, as well as those in common use in Palestine, had 'graven images' stamped upon them and were thereby an abomination in the eyes of the Lord. But the moneychangers frequently took advantage of their position and forced dubious exchange rates on the pious, particularly those who could least afford it. So notorious was the practice that it was not unusual for an aspiring politician to force the market down with a flood of holy currency to the raucous applause of the assembly.

The outer courtyard also housed the stalls of the sacrificial merchants; dealers in blood who brought lambs and birds tethered and in cages for holy sacrifice on the Temple altars. Invariably, on an occasion such as a Passover when the demand was great prices soared and again the hardest hit were the pious and the poor.

The outer courtyard was cacophonous with argument and the cries of animals, and reeked of the cloying stench of live things unnaturally penned under the hot, sharp dust of noon. Into this great enclosure, bright with the glare of white linen and the gleam of burnished armour, Jesus strode with his bodyguard like a prophet of old. He seized the nearest tables heaped with coins and hurled them to the ground. Two or three of the disciples grabbed tethering ropes from the animals and began to lay about them. Others released pigeons and doves or smashed their cages on the cobblestones. The courtyard erupted with cries of outrage, the terror-filled bleating of lambs, the sudden panicked bellow of calves. But above it all the shouts of Yesu'a, the ringleader, filled with the power wrought from a hundred open-air meetings in Galilee, ranged across the enclosure:

'Is it not written, "My house shall be called a house of prayer for all the nations?" But you have made it a den of robbers!'[2]

Time and again perhaps, the cry rang out and was answered with approval from the crowd who had followed him and from the poor he had found there. The anguished protests of the stall holders were to no avail in the face of such numbers.

But the act of destruction was short-lived. Jesus could not afford to allow it to become more than a symbolic occasion. If it turned into a serious outrage the Temple authorities would have their excuse to seize him and deal with him summarily.

In any case, it was unnecessary to go to such lengths. The symbolism of his actions was more than sufficient to attain his ends. He had shown himself to be a man of the people, a champion of the downtrodden, and they—his own kind—would listen to his words and understand his message.

He had taken his challenge to the Sanhedrin to the very steps of the Temple and in doing so had declared his own responsibility for the spiritual welfare of this holy of holies in the Judaic faith. One could scarcely imagine a more provocative act to an aristocratic Sadducee.

He had protected himself still further by increasing both the public interest in his activities and the size of the crowd which surrounded him.

The Sanhedrin's leaders must have been taken aback once again by the man's audacity. For the second time in two days he had violated the peace. It was almost as though he had thrown out a deliberate challenge to their authority.

But the Sanhedrin knew from experience the risk Jesus was running, even if he was unaware of it. They knew of old the fickleness of crowds, and that one thing was certain above all others: once he proclaimed himself the Messiah with words, as opposed to symbolic actions, they would have him. Notwithstanding the anguished howls of the poor and the crippled who sought an end to their misery in the great apocalypse, the more substantial citizens of the capital and the wealthy pilgrims, to whom messianism was no more than a pious dream, would rise and curse him for his blasphemy. A man standing before them in the flesh proclaiming a special relationship with the God whose name was so sacred it could never be uttered would be an outrage to them. And for this man to make the claim, this malformed associate of harlots and drunks, was criminally sacrilegious. They would as soon suffer forever under the Roman heel than believe that God would choose such a one as His messenger.

The course of action the Sanhedrin had decided on was not only correct but was bound to be effective. With their experience and their ready allies in the populace they would turn the upstart's crowds against him.

According to Mark, when Jesus left the Temple grounds he stayed in the city until evening and then departed once more for Bethany. No mention is made of his activities immediately following the incident in the Temple but it would be surprising if he had not used the opportunity to preach his apocalyptic message and the demand for repentance.

It was not until the following day—traditionally the Tuesday of the final week—that the Sanhedrin's agents were able to heckle him from the body of the crowd with their meticulously prepared questions.

Jesus was once again in the vicinity of the Temple and surrounded, we may imagine, by a considerable crowd: the disciples, the poor and the crippled, the moral pariahs and the urchins of the city, but also a goodly proportion of pilgrims anxious to see the man whose behaviour they had heard so much about. The merely curious of Jerusalem would also be represented and along with them the wealthy and the devout led there to be scarified by their guilt. The Sanhedrin's agents would have spread themselves through this multitude.

More than likely, the essence of Jesus' teaching was no different from what it had always been—the imminence of the New Kingdom, the need to repent—but in the minds of his audience the incidents of the last two days must have been paramount. So when the heckling broke out from a section of the crowd it applied to both his teaching and to these activities.

'By what authority are you doing these things?' they cried. 'Who gave you the authority to do them?'[3]

Perhaps the speaker ignored them at first to gain a breathing space; perhaps he was already well prepared. But in either case he could not have failed to be aware of the danger inherent in the questions. Clearly, they were a demand that he declare his relationship with his Heavenly Father. But if he did that, he knew, the reaction would be instantaneous. No man in a crowd could stand before a speaker and hear with equanimity the truth of the matter. But to deny his Father was unthinkable. There was only one solution and it was a quintessentially Jewish one. He answered a question by asking one. And in so doing he reaffirmed his relationship with his early mentor, the Baptist.

'I will ask you a question,' he said to the hecklers, 'answer me, and I will tell you by what authority I do these things.'

Perhaps the murmuring of the people hushed. The drama of the moment would not be lost on a crowd to whom oratorical by-play occupied so much of their lives.

'Was the baptism of John from heaven or from men? Answer me.'

It was the perfect riposte. For, says Mark, they argued with one another, 'If we say, "From heaven," he will say, "Why then did you not believe him?" But shall we say "From men"?' That was equally fraught since, as Mark reports, 'They were afraid of the people for all held that John was a real prophet.'

Their only alternative was the lame, 'We do not know'; the laughter which must have erupted from Jesus' followers would have been difficult to bear. Jesus was quick to capitalise on it. 'Neither will I tell you by what authority I do these things.'[4]

Thus relieved of the hecklers, says Mark, Jesus began to speak in parables. But they were not so easily put aside. Regathering their forces they challenged him with the second of the barbed demands:

> 'Teacher, we know that you are true, and care for no man; for you do not regard the position of men, but truly teach the way of God. Is it lawful to pay taxes to Caesar, or not? Should we pay them or should we not?'

Again, it seems, there was a hesitation before Jesus' substantive reply. 'Why put me to the test?' he asked. Perhaps he was again seeking time to formulate the reply, or perhaps knowing instantly what he must say, he was allowing the excitement to build within the crowd in the manner of all good orators. Finally, he called for a coin. Someone—possibly Judas, his treasurer—handed him a denarius. Holding it up to his opponents he called: 'Whose likeness and inscription is this?'

'Caesar's,' they replied.

He acknowledged the truth of it. Then he said, "Render to Caesar the things that are Caesar's and to God the things that are God's.'

And, says Mark, they were amazed at him.[5]

Well they might have been, for it was more than a clever oratorical trick. On the surface he might have been thought to be speaking simply of a division of loyalty between state and religion, and if he were challenged that interpretation was certainly available to him. But it was more significant than that. The denarius carried Caesar's image but it also bore the inscription 'Tiberius Caesar Divi: Divine Caesar'. Yet this blasphemous rendering was permitted by the Sanhedrin to circulate freely throughout Palestine, a constant reminder to the people of the council's preparedness to cooperate with the 'divine' oppressor. No one in the crowd could have failed to see beneath the bland parry and feel the sting in the riposte.

So, by his answer not only had Jesus neutralised the attack against him, but he had turned it back on his opponents. Once more the jeers of his supporters would have lashed the ears of the scribes and Pharisees.

The final question remained to be fired at him and, according to Mark, it was not long in coming.

'Teacher,' one shouted, 'Moses wrote for us that if a man's brother dies and leaves a wife, but leaves no child, the man may take the wife and raise up children for his brother. There were seven brothers; the first took a wife and when he died left no children; the second took her and died, leaving no children and the third likewise and the seven left no children. Last of all, the woman also died. In the resurrection whose wife will she be? For the seven had her as wife.'

The parallels between the question and the actual situation as it pertained to Herod Antipas are plain. Though it was couched in hypothetical and rather long-winded terms, it certainly invited Jesus to uphold or to deny the attitude of John the Baptist in whose shadow he so often seems to have walked.

But as such it was an outright failure. The questioner had outsmarted himself. In seeking to bury the barb deep in the bait he permitted his intended victim to bite off only as much as he needed and to ignore the rest. Jesus declined to be drawn in and in place of an answer delivered a miniature lecture on angelic theology and scriptural analysis:

> 'Is not this why you are wrong, that you know neither the scriptures nor the power of God? For when they rise from the dead, they neither marry nor are given in marriage but are like angels in heaven [asexual]. And as for the dead being raised, have you not read in the book of Moses in the passage about the bush, how God said to him, "I am the God of Abraham, and the God of Isaac, and the God of Jacob"? He is not the God of the dead but of the living; you are quite wrong.'[6]

Thus humiliated, the lordly Saducean interrogator (Mark specifically designates him a Sadducee) may be imagined to have held his peace thereafter.

The questioning was done. For the third time in three days Jesus had triumphed over his adversaries.

It is difficult to present in detail the sequence of events in the last week and while it suits a dramatic retelling to arrange the questions in Mark's order as just related, there can be no certainty that it is true to history. All that can be said with confidence is that at some stage during the week all three questions were put and their vigorous replies recorded and delighted in.

But while they reveal a continuing triumph for Jesus there can be no suggestion that his impact on the city caused the hundreds of thousands gathered there to swim to his banner.

Jerusalem was an old and skeptical city. It had watched prophets come and go for centuries and had usually sped them on their way with a hail of angry stones. Its attitude to Jesus was little different. Undeniably, he was permitted his share of attention, even a measure of fame among the ne'er-do-wells, but his impact cannot be rated much higher than that. It was sufficient to engage the spleen of the Sanhedrin and to fire their determination to destroy him but the city was far too world-weary to allow itself to be stormed by a mystical Nazarene, however impassioned his message or urgent his plea.

It has often been said that this inability of Jesus to inspire the citizenry of Jerusalem to acknowledge the truth of his cause constituted the second failure of his preaching career, the first being when Galilee failed to rise at the call of his disciples. It has also been said that this second, more devastating failure forced him to the extreme course of voluntary crucifixion as a final resort to 'prove' his identity.

The thesis has much to commend it. It is certainly not incompatible with the hypothesis that Jesus carried within his thoughts a plan he believed had been delivered to him by his Heavenly Father for the redemption of mankind and that he followed that plan as faithfully as he was able. For while he may have believed long before he reached Jerusalem that the climax of his mission would be as a sacrificial lamb on a Roman cross he must surely have hoped and prayed that he would be spared the final suffering: that it might be otherwise, that his Father might show him mercy and so illuminate the minds of all his listeners that the final act would become unnecessary. Might not his Father know that in his heart he was willing to make the supreme sacrifice, and if he were a God who knew a man's heart and cared little for the external panoply, might that not be sufficient?

Whatever he may have hoped the hard fact as he saw it was that his Father did not intervene with a sign which would transform the multitudes of Jerusalem into the sheep of his fold. The responsibility remained his alone. He must see it through to the end.

In three days he had accomplished much. For those who had eyes to see and ears to hear he had made his message plain. But they were a mere handful. His charge encompassed the whole of Israel and it was clear that they could not be reached without his taking the final dramatic step. He would surrender himself to the Sanhedrin; but, as always, he would remain in control. It would be at a time and place of his own choosing, not theirs. It would be so arranged that he would be allowed two further days to preach and prepare himself; and in the fulfilment of prophecy no blood would be shed at the time of his capture, no innocent onlookers harmed in the divine cause.

To accomplish this he had to enlist the services of his young intimate, Judas, who would be called upon to play a vital part in the final drama; a part which has been so misunderstood by Christianity that the young associate's very name has become a curse in all the languages of Christendom. It is, I suspect, one of the truly great injustices of history.

Notes

1. Luke 19:40—I am indebted to H.J. Schonfield's pioneering work The Passover Plot throughout this chapter, though I disagree with some of his interpretations.
2. Mark 11:17-18.
3. Mark 11:28.
4. Mark 11:29-33.
5. Mark 12:14-17.
6. Mark 12:18-27.

14

Judas

THE belief that Judas was the quintessential traitor of history—the betrayer of the Lord—is, to say the least, deeply entrenched, so deeply, in fact, that the name itself is often used to denote not the historical figure but traitorous behaviour per se. In these circumstances it would seem folly to put forward a different interpretation of the disciple's actions from the one traditionally accepted. But it must be done, for an undogmatic reading of the evidence points in a quite different direction.

It is clear, for example, that the gospel writers themselves were confused and unsure about the nature of the relationship between the disciple and his Master. In Mark there is no assertion at all of any motive in the betrayal. To reach even a tentative conclusion regarding Judas' motives one must rely on the order of the narrative. By the proximity of the passage it might be inferred that Judas was angered by Jesus' action in allowing a woman to anoint him with a costly jar of oil. It might have been that Judas was among the disciples who said: 'Why was the ointment thus wasted? For this ointment might have been sold for more than three hundred denarii, and given to the poor.'[1] But if that is the case we are asked to accept that Judas in his betrayal was fired by compassion for the poor, a rare motive indeed for murder. It becomes even more difficult to accept when the man against whom his anger is supposed to have been directed is Jesus of Nazareth, the champion of the poor and the downtrodden.

Then, according to Mark, Judas went to the chief priests 'in order to betray him to them. And when they heard it they were glad, and promised to give him money. And he sought an opportunity to betray him'.[2]

The significance of this passage lies in the fact that it was the chief priests, and not Judas, who raised the question of money. Judas, it is said, went there expressly 'in order to betray him'. The question of money did not arise until the chief priests mentioned it. And even then, they did not part with any but simply 'promised' it to him. Mark does not even bother to record whether or not it was ever paid.

Perceiving the weakness of the Marcan passage and seeking to clarify the matter to his own satisfaction, the author of Matthew changes the colloquy between Judas and the chief priests quite radically. Now instead of the priests offering to give him money after the betrayal Matthew reverses the order. He has Judas seeking some reward before the event. But in doing so he makes a quite transparent error, for he writes, 'Then one of the twelve, who was called Judas Iscariot, went to the chief priests and said, "What will you give me if I deliver him to you?" And they paid him thirty pieces of silver'.[3]

If the new scenario is to be preferred, we must accept two quite extraordinary propositions. First, that someone was present to record and make available to the author of Matthew the direct quotation, 'What will you give me if I deliver him to you?' Surely, that can be discounted? Secondly, that the chief priests were so naive as to part with their thirty pieces of silver before the 'betrayer' had completed his contract.

But the really damning evidence of Matthew's revision is contained in the very detail which seems to bring the encounter to life and to validate it: the declaration that the sum paid was 'thirty pieces of silver', a phrase almost as infamous as its alleged recipient. If his revision is a mere invention, where, we may ask, did he come by the notion that the sum involved was thirty silver shekels? Fortunately, the answer is not hard to find. As we have seen, Matthew has an extraordinary need to show that every element in the life of his subject 'fulfilled prophecy' by reference to the Old Testament. In this endeavour, one of his favourite references is the book of Zechariah; and in this instance Zechariah did not let him down. The passage he used is a mythical conversation between the prophet and Yahweh concerning Zechariah's dealings with the hated purveyors of sacrificial lambs, the merchants of blood:

> Then I [Zechariah] said to them, 'If it seems right to you, give me my wages; but if not, keep them.' And they weighed out as my wages thirty shekels of silver. Then the Lord said to me, 'Cast it into the treasury'—the lordly price at which I was paid off by them. So I took the thirty shekels of silver and cast them into the treasury in the house of the Lord. Then I broke my second staff Union, *annulling the brotherhood between Judah and Israel*.[4] [Italics mine]

The sum was thus perfect for Matthew's purposes, revealed in the gospels for all to see, the contemptible thirty shekels, the blood money, the payoff. So plainly is the passage an invention by Matthew and so clear its antecedent that even Luke shies away from it. The thirty shekels are simply not mentioned. However, Luke also recognises the problem of ascribing to Judas the implied Marcan motive of compassion for the poor, and the story of the costly oil is placed elsewhere and given no significance in the act.

But for once his well-recorded inventiveness lets him down and he is unable to find an alternative motive. Instead he is forced back upon the ultimate refuge of the apologist, the assertion that, 'Satan entered into Judas called Iscariot, who was of the number of the twelve'.

Luke totally rejects Matthew's version of the meeting between Judas and the chief priests. According to Luke, 'He went away and conferred with the chief priests and captains how he might betray him to them'.

It is only then that the question of money arises. 'And they were glad, and engaged to give him money. So he agreed, and sought an opportunity to betray him to them in the absence of the multitude'.[5]

The fourth gospel, written further from the event, makes use of both Luke's Satanic theory and Matthew's notion of avarice as the chief motivating factor. But in John's hands neither explanation is satisfactory. In each case the reference reads more like an afterthought than a significant element of the narrative, and in the case of the Satanic theory he appears to contradict his own rendering.

For instance, the gospel begins the story of the Third Passover with the words:

> Now before the feast of the Passover when Jesus knew that his hour had come to depart out of this world to the Father, having loved his own who were in the world, he loved them to the end. And during supper, when the devil had already put it into the heart of Judas Iscariot, Simon's son, to betray him, Jesus…rose from supper, laid aside his garments, and girded himself with a towel…[6]

Yet, later in the meal and just prior to Judas leaving to organise the betrayal, John says, 'so when he dipped the morsel he (Jesus) gave it to Judas, the son of Simon Iscariot. Then, after the morsel, Satan entered into him'. It is hard to imagine why Satan should have needed to enter Judas twice, particularly since no mention is made of his leaving in between.

John's version of Matthew's revision is just as suspect as the original. John is the only gospel writer to identify the woman who anointed Jesus with the costly oil as Mary, the sister of Lazarus.[7] In this respect his version may be more accurate than the synoptics. However, he is also the only writer to identify Judas as the one (and only) disciple who protests: 'Why was this ointment not sold for three hundred denarii and given to the poor?' Then, in a blatant editorial comment, the author says, 'This he said, not that he cared for the poor but because he was a thief, and as he had the money box he used to take what was put into it'.[8] The writer would have his readers believe that Jesus appointed a thief to be his treasurer, in charge of the funds which would otherwise have been distributed to the poor. The idea refutes itself by its silliness.

But curiously, John does not link Judas' thievery directly to the betrayal. He simply remarks, when identifying the disciple as the one who protested at the extravagance, that Judas Iscariot was 'he who was to betray him'. The direct cause, according to John, was Satan who 'entered' the unfortunate disciple (twice). Thus the gospel writers were not only confused in their treatment of the forces supposedly impelling Judas but contradictory as well. The situation does not improve in subsequent passages concerning the betrayal itself.

Mark says that during the Last Supper Jesus made the startling announcement to the disciples that one of them would betray him and 'they began to be sorrowful, and to say to him, one after another, "Is it I?"'

Jesus answered, 'It is one of the twelve, one who is dipping bread into the dish with me.'[9]

There is no suggestion, however, that he identifies the betrayer. On the contrary, the meal resumes and Jesus conducts the original of what would become known as the Eucharist, offering them all the bread as his body and the wine as his blood.

It is difficult to accept that after such a momentous statement the meal proceeded as before. In fact, the only saving grace to the story is that the other versions are even more incredible.

Matthew repeats the Marcan version verbatim but for one extraordinary addition. When Judas asks, 'Is it I, Master?' Jesus replies, 'You have said so.'[10]

But still, we are asked to believe the meal proceeded calmly—and this in a room full of frightened, emotionally overwrought followers asking in horror, one after the other, who would be the one to betray their Master!

Luke rejects the earlier version and seems to gloss over the incident. According to this version, Jesus is in the middle of the Eucharist when he appears to break off the ceremony immediately after breaking the bread and passing it around. 'But behold,' Jesus says, 'the hand of him who betrays me is with me on the table. For the Son of Man goes as it has been determined; but woe to that man by whom he is betrayed!'

Then, says Luke, 'they began to question one another which of them it was that would do this'. But the argument is apparently short-lived since the next sentence relates: 'A dispute also arose among them, which of them was to be regarded as the greatest…'

Jesus pacifies them and then in a most remarkable passage says, 'I assign to you, as my Father assigned to me, a kingdom, that you may eat and drink at my table in my kingdom, and sit on thrones judging the twelve tribes of Israel.'[11]

How Jesus could at once damn his betrayer and in the next breath appoint him to a throne to judge one of the tribes of

Israel cannot be rationalised by Christian apologists, however they contort themselves. But it is left to the fourth gospel to deliver the most bewildering version. For according to John, the Beloved Disciple is intimately involved in the accusation during the Last Supper. The passage bears repeating in full:

> When Jesus had thus spoken he was troubled in spirit, and testified, 'Truly, truly, I say to you, one of you will betray me.' The disciples looked at one another, uncertain of whom he spoke. One of his disciples, whom Jesus loved, was lying close to the breast of Jesus; so Simon Peter beckoned to him and said, 'Tell us who it is of whom he speaks.' So lying thus, close to the breast of Jesus, he said to him, 'Lord, who is it?' Jesus answered, 'It is he to whom I shall give this morsel when I have dipped it.' So when he had dipped the morsel he gave it to Judas, the son of Simon Iscariot. Then, after the morsel, Satan entered into him. Jesus said to him, 'What you are going to do, do quickly.'[12]

It would seem to any reasonable reader that with the betrayer having been identified so unequivocally, a terrible uproar must surely ensue. But according to John this is not the case.

Now no one at the table knew why he said this to him. Some thought that, because Judas had the money box Jesus was telling him, 'Buy what we need for the feast'; [despite the all-too-obvious fact that the feast was actually in progress] or, that he should give something to the poor. So, after receiving the morsel he immediately went out; and it was night.[13]

There are similar discrepancies in the four versions of Judas' appearance with the soldiers at the Garden of Gethsemane.

According to Mark, Judas identifies Jesus for the soldiers with a kiss and Jesus acquiesces to 'fulfil the scriptures'.[14]

Matthew, ever the elaborator, has Jesus say to Judas immediately after the kiss, 'Friend, why are you here?'—in itself a remarkable statement since according to the same author Jesus was quite aware of the man's purpose.[15]

Luke would have it that Jesus drew back, declining Judas's embrace with the words, 'Judas, would you betray the Son of Man with a kiss?' before surrendering himself without a struggle to the authorities.[16]

According to John, Jesus sees the group of soldiers coming and goes to them saying, 'Whom do you seek?' And they answered, 'Jesus of Nazareth.' Jesus said to them, 'I am he.'

Judas, who had betrayed him, was standing with them. When he said to them, 'I am he' they drew back and fell to the ground. Again, he asked them, 'Whom do you seek?' And they said, 'Jesus of Nazareth.' Jesus answered, 'I told you that I am he; so if you seek me, let these men go.'[17]

After a small scuffle during which one of the high priests' slaves has his ear cut off (which, according to Luke, was miraculously replaced by Jesus) the Nazarene surrenders and is led away.

The only other appearance of Judas in the gospels is in Matthew where Judas is said to have repented his crime and returned the mythical thirty pieces of silver…'and he went and hanged himself'.[18]

The priests use the money to buy a potter's field in which to bury foreigners, the place becoming known as the Field of Blood. According to Matthew, this was done 'to fulfil prophecy'.

In the Acts of the Apostles, however, the author (probably Luke) has Judas himself buy the field and brings the betrayer to an even less savoury death...'falling headlong he burst open in the middle and all his bowels gushed out'.[19]

This is very much in the vein of later apocryphal works which assign all manner of horrendous deaths to the disciple and in doing so reveal a taste for cruelty endemic to the religions of the Middle East, Christianity chief among them, to a quite horrifying extent. In this respect, it is interesting that in Moslem polemic literature Judas is not portrayed as a traitor; instead, he is said to have lied to the Jews to protect Jesus (who himself was not crucified). The 10th century historian, al-Tabari of Baghdad, even asserts that Judas assumed the likeness of Jesus and attempted to have himself crucified in his place. Moreover, he says that this is the opinion of some Christians as well. This could be so since the apocryphal Gospel of Judas, written in the 2nd century, denies his guilt. However, only fragments of this gospel have survived.

But it seems unnecessary to rely on apocrypha or Moslem tradition to cast the most serious doubts on the historicity of Judas' betrayal. The gospels themselves are sufficient.

Recognising this, orthodox scholars have gone to extraordinary lengths to try to meld the differing versions and to suggest alternative motivations for the 'betrayal'. It has been said, for example, that Iscariot should not be translated in the usual manner as 'man of Kerioth' a town of Palestine, but as a corruption of Sicarii, a group of Jewish radicals sometimes aligned with the Zealots and who regarded it as their duty to assassinate Roman officials at every opportunity. On this reading, Judas would have as a surname 'assassin' or 'murderer'—a description of his nature rather than his place of birth.

Also, it has been said that since both Judas and his father were Zealots who believed in a secret political Messiah, Jesus may well have disappointed them by rejecting the idea of a violent revolution; so much so that the son was willing to hand the Master over for crucifixion. If this were so, it is curious that the father was not similarly involved but instead, despite the horrific nature of his son's actions, apparently remained a disciple in good standing after the crucifixion.

In all, the rationalisations which involve an acceptance of Judas as a traitor, whether from political, personal or criminal motives are as little convincing as the various gospel stories. The one factor which all have failed to take into account is the manner by which Jesus conducted what he believed was a divine plan which would bring about the New Kingdom of God.

Despite the evidence of the gospels, there has been little recognition of the fact that he told his various followers only as much as was necessary for them to carry out their part of the plan. Thus, among other things, he was able to arrange for the ass to be waiting, for the house of the Last Supper to be available; thus he was able to develop a relationship with Nicodemus and Joseph of Arimathea and the Beloved Disciple all without the knowledge of the Galilean disciples as revealed by the synoptic gospels.

To such a leader it would be natural to confide only in a young favourite whom he had brought into his intimate circle, a zealot in the modern sense of the term, to carry out the single most important function of his final week on earth—his delivery, peacefully and without bloodshed, into the hands of his enemies so that at last the greatest prophecy of all would be fulfilled.

That he told no one else, and that he swore Judas to secrecy, follows equally naturally. For if the other disciples were to learn of it, the plan would have been shattered. Some would have fled (as in fact all did when he was taken); others would have damned the mad folly of it; still others would have raised arms with misguided zeal to defend him against himself. In short, he would have lost control over his activities at the most fateful time. And that was the element which had to be protected at all costs. He and he alone must remain in charge. The plan must be protected. No one else must know of Judas' mission. The secret must be kept.

On the evidence, he was successful.

Notes

1. Mark 14:3-5.
2. Mark 14:10.
3. Matthew 26:14-15.
4. Zechariah 11:12.
5. Luke 22:4-6.
6. John 13:1-5.
7. John 13:26-27.
8. John 12:5-6.
9. Mark 14:20-21.
10. Matthew 26:25.
11. Luke 22:21-30.
12. John 13:21-28.
13. John 13:28-30.
14. Mark 14:49.
15. Matthew 26:50.
16. Luke 22:48.
17. John 18:4-8.
18. Matthew 27:3-6.
19. Acts 1:18-19.

15

The Last Days

AT Jesus' behest, probably on the Wednesday of the final week, Judas went to the chief priests with his offer to deliver the Galilean into their hands. To the Sanhedrin it must almost have seemed that their prayers had been answered. Frustrated by Jesus' tactics in surrounding himself with a multitude during the day and retreating to Bethany in the evening, angered by his ability to turn their heckling—and the crowds—against them, it must have seemed to the leaders that they would be forced to go cap in hand to Pilate with a request for soldiers to take the cursed Nazarene. But once they did that they handed the Procurator a weapon which he would be delighted to use against them. They would acknowledge their dependence upon him. Thereafter, any appeal over his head to Caesar for greater autonomy would be laughed out of court.

Little wonder then that they received Judas with 'gladness' and sought to cement the bargain with the promise of a reward.

It is not difficult to imagine Judas returning to his Master, exhilarated at having accomplished the first part of his mission yet fearful of its consequences. For he was engaged in an endeavour which must at times have seemed unreal to him. That he, Judas of Kerioth, should be the key to the drama which would bring about the end of the world and, at the side of his Master, usher in the New Kingdom of God, was almost impossible to contemplate. Yet that was precisely what was about to happen. Jesus had said so. It must be true.

Judas's return marked another step on the path Jesus had chosen. The door was closing behind him. Soon there would be no way back. But at least he had assured himself of one more day, a day he would spend in Bethany at his devotions and in the hills beyond the town walking alone the way he had as a youth in Galilee, feeling the blessed warmth of the sun and silently communing with his Father, preparing himself for that awesome moment when at last they would meet.

If he slept that night it could only have been briefly; when the first wash of colour swept in from the east. Yesu'a, 'The Help of Yahweh', was more than likely waiting for it, glad that his time had almost come.

It was the first day of Unleavened Bread and there were important ceremonies which must be observed. First among them was the sacrifice of the Passover Lamb which his disciples and the rest of the company brought to him. The dedication must surely have had a special poignancy for him, the innocent lamb a symbol of the reality which was to follow.

At the end of it, says Mark, his disciples came to him with the request, 'Where will you have us go and prepare for you to eat the Passover?'

His answer was immediate.

> 'Go into the city and a man carrying a jar of water will meet you; follow him and wherever he enters, say to the householder, "The Teacher says, where is my guest room, where I am to eat the Passover with my disciples?" And he will show you a large upper room furnished and ready; there prepare for us.'[1]

Again, the plan was unfolding. Again, Jesus was taking care that nothing would interfere with its realisation. The man carrying the water jar would be impossible for the disciples to miss, for men simply did not carry water—that was a job for women. The only conceivable impediment was that the man might draw unwanted attention to himself. But that was a risk which had to be taken and, in the scheme of things, an acceptable one.

There can be no certainty about who owned the house. There has been speculation among scholars that it was Nicodemus or Joseph of Arimathea. But, as has been mentioned, since neither of them attended the Last Supper—and it is highly unlikely that the owner would not have been present—the weight of evidence suggests that the house belonged to the Beloved Disciple and, if the fourth gospel is to be credited, it is the same house to which he took Mary, Jesus' mother, following the crucifixion. Certainly, it seems, the Beloved Disciple sat at the place of honour 'close to the breast of Jesus' throughout the meal.

The Last Supper itself has been the subject of minute examination and wide disparity of interpretation among Christians over many centuries. Its central feature is the celebration of the Eucharist when, according to the synoptics, Jesus personalised the traditional Passover meal by speaking of the wine as his blood and the bread as his body.

There seems little reason to doubt that something of the kind took place and that it made a deep impression upon those present. It quickly became the custom of the early Church to 'commune' with Jesus and to remember the occasion in a formalised breaking of bread and drinking of communal wine in the Essenic tradition. Indeed, to the apostle Paul the ceremonial became the central physical affirmation of the faith.

It is significant that in the telling none of his female followers were involved. By the time the gospels reached their present form, it seems, male censors had all but expunged women from the story. It is ironic, though by no means untypical, that the ceremony which Paul spoke of as a great uniting force among Christians—'Because there is one bread, we who are many are one body'—became the cause of so much disunity among contending schisms, bloodshed and gender exclusion.

The gospels themselves have contributed to the problem by the variety of their versions; the fourth gospel ignoring it altogether, and there can be little doubt that within the synoptics, copyists and editors have 'clarified' the text to suit their own ends.

But the essential nature of the gathering is not in doubt. To Jesus, as to all Jews, the Passover was the holiest of all the celebrations in the Mosaic calendar, the affirmation of Israel as the chosen nation of God, the remembrance of the covenant. It was proper then, that the momentous events about to take place should do so within that holy time. More than merely proper, it was necessary to the plan and an essential ingredient within it.

But there was more to the gathering than adherence to the presumed divine formula. Jesus and the disciples had ventured into the city at night for the first time since their arrival in Jerusalem. They were in the enemy camp, vulnerable to the Sanhedrin's spies and sudden arrest. For the disciples, who knew nothing of the bargain Judas had concluded with the chief priests, it must have been a nerve-racking occasion. Not even Jesus could be sure that the Annas faction would honour its commitment and await his voluntary surrender.

In a deeply human sense, it was the last meal Jesus would share with his closest and most faithful followers. They had shared so much: the earliest times when they must have resembled a travelling sideshow; the growing popularity as news of his 'cures' spread to the villages and country towns; the pain of rejection when Galilee refused to respond to the disciples' mighty proclamations; the terrible times when the wine became a balm and a release; the bickering and the jealousy which he had to keep tethered when their crude, unlettered minds began to play with the concept of the New Kingdom and its spoils; the rivalries and affection and love which had to be controlled and channelled as much as he was able...all of these elements must have been present as he sat with them and began the Seder.

It fell to Jesus as Rabbi to make the ancient incantation over the first of the four obligatory cups of wine before passing it on for them to share. At such a time, knowing it was the last, knowing that soon he would be leaving them to pursue alone the final phase of the course he had charted, it would have been extraordinary if he had not spoken of his love for them and his fear that they would desert him.

Equally, in the emotion of the moment, it is understandable that Peter should have protested: 'Even though they all fall away I will not.' And it is simplicity itself to see Jesus, knowing the faint-heartedness of the former fisherman, reproaching him with the words, 'Truly, I say to you, this very night, before the cock crows twice, you will deny me.'[2]

As well, there was the Beloved Disciple beside him, affectionate as always, leaning close to his breast and speaking in whispers; and a little way off, Judas, whose eyes never left him, awaiting the signal to leave and to complete the most hazardous part of his mission.

And when he judged the time to be right he would have beckoned Judas to him and as he came within earshot said, 'What you have to do, do quickly.'[3]

Now it was time to leave. He must go to Gethsemane as arranged—the place where, we are told, he and his disciples often paused on their way back to Bethany in the evenings. It was a short walk from the house across the Kidron Valley to the tree-shadowed garden and he hurried there with Peter, James and John.

Once they had reached Gethsemane there was little for them to do but wait with him, ignorant of what was to follow. It must have seemed strange, erratic behaviour on Jesus' part, the more so since he asked them to remain a little way off from him while he sought confirmation one last time that the course he had chosen was the one which his Father required of him.

Soon the wine they had drunk at the supper began to take effect. They dozed and Jesus returned from his prayers to find them sleeping. 'Simon,' he said, reverting to the formalism of Peter's given name, 'are you asleep? Could you not watch one hour?'[4]

It is a poignant and wholly convincing anecdote. One can almost feel with Peter the awfulness of his recollection, that on the last occasion they were together Jesus had been obliged to reproach him. He had let the Master down.

When Judas appeared with the Sanhedrin's armed band Jesus calmed his followers as the disciple approached. Judas went to him and, for the last time, kissed him. The others, astonished at the sudden turn of events may well have attempted to protect him but Jesus was adamant. No blood must be shed. The scriptures must be fulfilled. And, says Mark, they all forsook him and fled. Even, it seems, the one who had nothing to fear from the Sanhedrin, Judas himself.

In Mark, there is the curious addendum to the episode not found in the other gospels. He writes, 'And a young man followed him, with nothing but a linen cloth about his body; and they seized him, but he left the linen cloth and ran away naked'.[5]

It is a tantalising passage and one which has not received much attention from orthodox Christian scholars. The reason is probably their concern to present only the Galilean aspect of Jesus' ministry to the exclusion of his Judaic mission.

However, it has been suggested by Schonfield in his respected 1965 work, 'The Passover Plot' that the young man was in fact the Beloved Disciple who had learned from his associates in the Temple of the imminent arrest of Jesus and had run to warn him, clad only in his nightclothes. While this explanation can be rated as not much more than a possibility it would at least help to explain how Jesus' followers were able to learn details of his interrogation and trial.

Only the Beloved Disciple was in a position to gain access to these events and to tell of his behaviour before the Sanhedrin. Certainly no Galileans were present.

So it may well have been that the young man, in a frenzy of fear for his Master, surrendered his cloak to the soldiers when they grabbed him and ran naked through the streets to his home before dressing and hurrying to the place where Jesus' ordeal was about to begin.

According to the fourth gospel, Jesus was escorted under armed guard to the man who led the faction of the Sanhedrin that was so totally opposed to the troublemaker from Nazareth: Annas, father-in-law of the Chief priest Caiaphas and head of the most powerful family in Jerusalem. Annas had himself been chief priest in previous years and had lobbied to secure the position for his son-in-law. He, more than any other, was working to have the northerner disposed of before he could destroy their plans for the ousting of Pilate and greater self-determination (and power for his own family) within the empire.

Resourceful and determined, Annas may well have seen in Jesus the opportunity to turn a potential embarrassment into a victory. To this end, perhaps, he worked to ensure that it was Pilate, and not the Sanhedrin who would be seen by the people to have killed the preacher. Jesus would have to be judged under the civil law of Rome, preferably by Pilate himself, so that if his death caused an insurrection the anger of the people and the resulting opprobrium of the Emperor would be directed at the Procurator.

But first he had to decide for himself the quality of the man he was dealing with. Obviously, there was more to him than the usual frenzied fanatic from Galilee. His tactics in arranging his entry to the city and the manner in which he had parried the carefully prepared questions of the scribes and Pharisees were enough to put anyone on his guard. Perhaps there were more surprises in store. Perhaps he was trying to lead the Sanhedrin into some elaborate trap. Annas had to know.

The questioning, which took place at the home of the high priest, was, we may believe, intense and prolonged. But all that has come down to us is a single reply from Jesus and even that is suspect in the hands of the anti-Semitic Elder from Ephesus. In response to a question from Annas 'about his disciples and his teaching', Jesus says:

> 'I have spoken openly to the world; I have always taught in synagogues and in the Temple, where all Jews come together; I have said nothing secretly. Why do you ask me? Ask those who heard me, what I said to them; they know what I said.'

Whereupon, we are told, one of the officers standing by struck Jesus with his hand saying, 'Is this how you answer the high priest?'[6]

Annas then sent him, bound, to the official residence of the chief priest, Caiaphas.

There is no record in John of any questioning by Caiaphas, though the synoptic gospels all strongly suggest that it was before Caiaphas rather than Annas that the main interrogation took place and that a procession of false witnesses arraigned themselves against Jesus.

Interestingly, one factor the two accounts have in common is that nowhere is it suggested that the so-called 'betrayer' Judas had any part to play in the proceedings. It is hardly to be credited that if he were in fact a traitor—whatever his motivation—that he would not also be the chief witness against the messianic pretender. He was, after all, not only one of the twelve intimates of the Preacher but treasurer of the band and in a perfect position to denounce him. Yet nothing is heard from him. He has vanished.

It is apparent that Caiaphas had called an extraordinary meeting of the Sanhedrin to hear the charges. In Mark, Jesus listens to the false and contradictory evidence without comment—'like a lamb that is led to the slaughter, and like a sheep that before its shearers is dumb, so he opened not his mouth'.

Only when one of the high priests challenges him to deny his special relationship with his Heavenly Father does Jesus break his silence. But when he does it is no timid admission of guilt but a firm declaration of his identity. He is the Messiah, and soon the world will see him 'sitting at the right hand of Power, and coming with the clouds of Heaven'.

The declaration enrages the Sanhedrin; 'the high priest tore his mantle, and said, "Why do we still need witnesses? You have heard his blasphemy. What is your decision?" And they all condemned him as deserving death. And some began to spit on him, and to cover his face, and to strike him, "Prophesy!" and the guards received him with blows'.[7]

It is clear then that the Sanhedrin condemned Jesus for his religious blasphemy. But the penalty for such a crime was not crucifixion but death by stoning. According to the fourth gospel Pilate himself had recently withdrawn the power of the Sanhedrin to impose a death sentence of any kind. If that is accepted—and there is no supporting evidence for it, either biblical or secular—it became necessary for the Sanhedrin to involve the Procurator in the proceedings. But equally, it may well have seemed to Annas that Pilate's involvement was essential if there were any possibility of protest from the citizens and pilgrims of Jerusalem. In that case he, and not they, would bear the brunt of the people's anger.

In fact, this seems the more likely explanation for, according to Mark, the Sanhedrin reassembled early in the morning for 'a consultation' before delivering him to Pilate. And when Pilate tells Jesus of the charges against him they have been radically changed. Now he is accused of styling himself 'the King of the Jews' and as such is a rebel against the State, a 'foe of Caesar'.

It is possible that here for the first time Jesus began to lose control over his fate. If he were to die by stoning—in the manner of prophets—his death would itself be a sign. But once the Sanhedrin shifted the responsibility to Pilate the barbarous practice of crucifixion was inevitable.

But in either case Jesus 'opened not his mouth' and accepted his fate. The Sanhedrin's tactic, if that is what it was, in forcing the Procurator to identify himself with the death of Jesus was successful. Finally, it was a Roman, the cruel, overbearing and corrupt Pontius Pilate, who sat in judgement on the Galilean.

It is one of the terrible ironies of history that in its wake would come Jewish persecution and bloodshed on a scale previously unknown on earth. The Annas faction's ploy served only to inflame the early apologists for the new faith and in their writings lay the foundation for limitless suffering. The charge that 'the Jews killed Christ' has echoed across twenty centuries of persecution and slaughter, culminating—if in fact it has yet done so—in the gas ovens of Christian Europe. And, as is the way of such things, the persecution has been all the more violent, the branding of Jews as 'Christ killers' all the more loudly proclaimed, because the accounts upon which the charges are based are at best uncertain and contradictory.

Notes

1. Mark 14:12-16.
2. Mark 14:29-30.
3. John 13:27.
4. Mark 14:37-38.
5. Mark 14:51-52.
6. John 18:20-23.
7. Mark 14:62-65.

16

The End

ACCORDING to Mark, the high priests took Jesus to Pilate immediately after their 'consultation' which had been held at first light ('as soon as it was morning').[1]

The hour is significant. From what little we know of Pilate's personal habits they did not lend themselves to early rising. Clearly, the priests were concerned to have the matter done without interference from the pilgrims and citizens of Jerusalem.

The charge, as we have seen, was that Jesus had declared himself 'the King of the Jews' and was thus a traitor to the State. If there was an element of messianism in the charge it was the broadest possible rendering of it. But it had the virtue of being both understandable to the Roman mind and of placing Jesus' 'crime' firmly under the purview of secular law.

Pilate, it seems, was suspicious of his political foes and their silent prisoner who could hardly have cut the figure of a truculent rebel. He had been dealing with the Sanhedrin for nine years and was aware of its members' prowess at political infighting. Perhaps this was just another trick to manoeuvre him into an embarrassing exchange with the Emperor, another tactic in their continuing battle of wits.

Pilate questions Jesus but receives no substantive reply. The priests redouble their efforts, heaping calumny upon slander until in exasperation Pilate shouts to the prisoner: 'Have you no answer to make?'

Jesus keeps his silence.

Apparently, reluctant to be drawn into the affair Pilate seeks refuge in the custom which allowed him to release a condemned prisoner each Passover. And in this the gospels are strangely illogical. All the accounts say the priests initiated the demand for the custom to be followed but all name the prisoner involved as Barabbas, the synoptics describing him as a murderer and the fourth gospel as a robber.

As all the gospels would have it, Pilate takes this opportunity to offer the release of Jesus but the priests instead call for Barabbas to be released. However, Jesus had not then been condemned. On the contrary, at that very moment Pilate was being implored by the crowd to condemn him. In those circumstances it simply makes no sense for him to offer Jesus' release as an act of grace in opposition to the crowd's demands.

Also, it would have been quite out of character for the high priests to request the release of a genuine rebel leader at a time when they were seeking the death of a political pacifist, however disagreeable his messianic pretensions.

It is far more likely that it was Pilate who took the initiative and that he, rather than the priests, introduced Barabbas into the equation. For if Pilate forced them into a choice between Jesus and Barabbas he immediately protected his own political standing with the Emperor. Whatever the Sanhedrin might say of him should anything untoward occur after the crucifixion of Jesus, he could always show that they had accepted the release of an armed rebel, a convicted murderer and insurrectionist, in preference to the Galilean. Only in that sense does the episode have any semblance of logicality, whatever its theological implications.

According to Mark, the Procurator then goes on to order Jesus' crucifixion.

Matthew follows the pattern set in Mark but with some imaginative additions. Pilate's wife, for instance, is said to have sent him a note during the trial, saying, 'Have nothing to do with that righteous man, for I have suffered much over him today in a dream.'[2] What little is known about Pilate's wife, a Roman aristocrat, well connected at Court, does not suggest she spent her nights dreaming about Jewish messiahs.

More important to the anti-Semites, Matthew's Pilate declines to sentence the prisoner and 'washes his hands' before the crowd, saying, 'I am innocent of this man's blood; see to it yourselves,'[3] though this is immediately contradicted as Matthew resumes the Marcan narrative.

But it is a dramatic and exculpatory action if it has any basis in fact. Pilate could be seen as no more than a misguided bumbler trapped by the Satanic forces of darkness as embodied in the Jewish religious leaders. However, once again—as with the thirty pieces of silver—Matthew's sources shine through. On this occasion it is Psalms 26:6: 'I wash my hands in innocence and go about thy altar, O Lord...'

Even more incredible is the response of the large crowd which, in Matthew, has gathered about the chief priests and officials to demand Jesus' death. As he would have it, they spontaneously proclaim: 'His blood be on us and on our children!'[4] It is difficult to imagine a more absurd proclamation or a more useful passage to the persecutors who would follow.

Luke declines to accept Matthew's additions but includes one of his own unrecorded elsewhere. According to the third gospel, the priests accuse Jesus before Pilate of 'perverting our nation, and forbidding us to give tribute to Caesar and saying that he himself is Christ, a king'.

Pilate: 'Are you the King of the Jews?'
Jesus: 'You have said so.'
Pilate: 'I find no crime in this man.'

But the priests are insistent and declare that he 'stirs up the people from Galilee to Jerusalem'.

Seizing on the mention of Galilee, Pilate sends the prisoner to Herod Antipas but the meeting is apparently inconclusive since Herod sends him back mocked and arrayed 'in gorgeous apparel'.[5]

Pilate again proposes to release him but the priests and the crowd will have none of it. Instead, Luke follows the earlier gospels' version of the Roman's ploy in offering the choice between Jesus and Barabbas for crucifixion. The crowd demands the release of the murderer and this is granted. But at least in Luke it is still Pilate who actively sits in judgement.

The fourth gospel, the most violently anti-Semitic of all, seeks to lay the blame (if blame there can be in a voluntary execution) as firmly as possible with 'the Jews'. To accomplish this, the author has expanded the scene considerably and it bears repeating in some detail.

Again, Jesus is led to the Praetorium at the west of the city early in the morning and Pilate is summoned.

Pilate: 'What accusation do you bring against this man?'

The Jews: 'If this man were not an evildoer we would not have handed him over.'

Pilate: 'Take him yourselves and judge him by your own law.'

The Jews: 'It is not lawful for us to put any man to death.'

Pilate (to Jesus): 'Are you the King of the Jews?' (A curious question, since in John there has been no mention of such a charge.)

Jesus: 'Do you say this of your own accord or did others say it to you about me?'

Pilate: 'Am I a Jew? *Your own nation* and the chief priests have handed you over to me. What have you done?' [Italics mine]

Jesus: 'My kingship is not of this world; if my kingship were of this world, *my servants would fight, that I might not be handed over to the Jews*; but my kingship is not from the world.' [Italics mine]

Pilate: 'So you are a king?'

Jesus: 'You say that I am a king. For this I was born and for this I have come into the world, to bear witness to the truth. Everyone who is of the truth hears my voice.'

Pilate: 'What is truth?'

The question apparently receives no significant reply and Pilate tells the Jews: 'I find no crime in him.' Then, the author of the fourth gospel says, Pilate offers to release Jesus but the crowd instead demand the release of Barabbas who in John 'was a robber'.

For no apparent reason Pilate then takes Jesus and scourges him, his soldiers mock him and again Pilate returns to the Jews: 'Behold, I am bringing him out to you, that you may know that I find no crime in him. Here is the man!' Jesus appears in a crown of thorns and a purple robe supplied by the soldiers.

'Crucify him, crucify him!' cry the Jews.

Pilate: 'Take him yourselves and crucify him, for I find no crime in him.'

The Jews: 'We have a law, and by that law he ought to die, because he has made himself the Son of God.'

According to John, Pilate is now 'more afraid'. He returns to Jesus: 'Where are you from?' (A curious question so late in the interrogation.)

Jesus declines to answer.

Pilate: 'You will not speak to me? Do you not know that I have power to release you, and power to crucify you?'

Jesus: 'You would have no power over me unless it had been given you from above; *therefore he who has delivered me to you has the greater sin.*' [Italics mine]

Once more, we are told, Pilate tries to release him but the Jews cry out: 'If you release this man you are not Caesar's friend; everyone who makes himself a king sets himself against Caesar.'

Pilate makes one more effort. He brings Jesus out, a small hunched figure, anything but the warlike revolutionary of their testimony. 'Behold,' says Pilate, 'your King.'

But the Jews apparently fail to grasp his irony. 'Away with him, away with him,' they cry. 'Crucify him!'

Pilate: 'Shall I crucify your King?'

The chief priests: 'We have no king but Caesar.'

Then, says John, Pilate handed Jesus over to the Jews to be crucified.[6]

The intention of the author could hardly be plainer. Here, for the first time, it is the Jews who run the crucifixion and who bear the whole responsibility.

So they took Jesus, and he went out, bearing his own cross to the place called the place of the skull which is called, in Hebrew, Golgotha. There they crucified him.

Only later in the account is it stated in self-contradiction, 'when the soldiers had crucified Jesus...' But the innocent reader would be in no doubt whatever that this was the story of a man being entrapped, even 'framed' by a group of bullies who used their shouts and implied threats to stampede a reluctant judge into a conviction. Yet on analysis this is a most unlikely scenario.

For all his faults, Pontius Pilate was not a man easily forced into precipitate action by his enemies in Jerusalem. On the contrary, the episode of the Temple funds is proof in itself that he was perfectly willing to stand up to them.

His actions in this case might be understandable, given the troublesome nature of his fief, if the demands of the Sanhedrin had been to spare someone he had condemned to death. Fear of a spontaneous uprising from the Passover crowd already angry at the earlier incident might have provided sufficient incentive for him to relent. But the gospel accounts suggest the contrary: that he was prepared to risk an uprising of the masses by agreeing to the demands of the ruling cabal for the death of a Galilean fanatic. Nowhere is it suggested that if he refused to crucify the man the masses would rise against him. Far from it. The gospels abound with references to the multitudes who followed Jesus about approving his victorious debates with the scribes and Pharisees.

Here, perhaps, lies the real significance of the Barabbas story. It has been misspoken and used by the gospel writers to show the lengths to which the Jews would go to secure the death of Jesus. In truth, it is much more likely that Pilate, having forced the choice between the two prisoners and having thus cleverly secured for himself protection against future imperial redress, was perfectly happy to send yet another deluded Jewish miracle worker to Golgotha. Had there been any serious doubts in his mind over the man's guilt, or had he seriously suspected the Sanhedrin of laying a trap, there was nothing to stop him throwing the fellow into prison for a few days and investigating the charges himself. Possibly such a course would have suited the more moderate members of the Sanhedrin as well. But according to the gospels, the idea simply did not occur to Pilate. Jesus just was not that important. Summary justice prevailed as a matter of course, just as it did with the two felons crucified on either side of him. A relatively small thing.

Not, however, to Jesus; for the essential element of his role in all the accounts is his active compliance in the course of events as they took place around him. Having declared himself the promised Messiah and having secured the condemnation of the cabal in the Sanhedrin, his one concern was to ensure that nothing would interfere with the realisation of his plan. And clearly, had he so chosen, there was ample opportunity for him to influence those events. For even if the accounts of Pilate's reluctance to condemn him are greatly exaggerated (as they certainly seem to have been) there can be little doubt that the Procurator was wary of the Sanhedrin's motives, concerned that he might be drawn into a trap. In those circumstances—and Jesus could hardly have been unaware of them—it would not have been difficult for him to have played on the Roman's fears and, at the very least, saved himself from the cross.

He made no attempt to do so. Instead, he allowed his silence, his passivity, to enrage and alienate the Roman activist. In doing so he not only turned Pilate against him but allied him with the priests. Natural enemies they might have been, but in the face of such contemptible, hangdog passivity, the positivists of the world unite. Pilate and the priests found common ground in Yesu'a, the victim.

Even when the trial was over and the death sentence passed, still Jesus kept silent. It may have been that no opportunity was given him to make the customary final statement. Certainly, there is a detectable air of urgency about the proceedings, a fear of interruption perhaps, which might have precluded the procedural norms. But had he wished to make a final testimony there can be little doubt that Pilate would have granted the indulgence.

But perhaps by then the world around him no longer possessed the reality it had once held for him; perhaps he was once more trapped inside himself, gripped in the belief that he was communing with his Heavenly Father, seeking and finding in that belief the strength to continue the ordeal. Perhaps there, at his core, he could find relief from the blows and the lashes which had punctuated the long hours of questioning. Perhaps there, in that strange pocket of the mind, he was touching the store of ecstasy he had found in his despair at Caesarea Philippi:

at the true and certain knowledge that he was his Father's son, the child of Yahweh, the Anointed One.

And his coronation was imminent.

DEATH

They led Jesus from the Procurator's palace through the winding streets of Jerusalem and out of the city towards Golgotha, the place of the skull. Though the fourth gospel makes no mention of it, the synoptics record that he was unable to carry the crossbeam of his cross and that a passerby, one Simon of Cyrene, was pressed into service.

It is a touching incident, of little theological importance but revealing all the same. The superhuman Jesus of John could be permitted no weakness. The synoptics are more down to earth. Also, as has been noted, the incident lends weight to the view that Jesus was by no means the perfect athletic figure of so many Renaissance paintings but a small man whose strength lay not in his physical form but in the intensity of his belief. But even that, it would seem, was insufficient to bear with grace the material of his execution.

According to the gospels, none of the Galilean disciples accompanied him on this last journey. They had apparently scattered at the news of his arrest and were still in hiding. It is tempting to speculate that Judas was there, following him through the crowd, shocked and horrified as the Master stumbled and was dragged roughly to his feet by the soldiers; tempting to believe that Judas was seized by a sudden terror that Jesus had lost control of the situation and that there was no escape, that the soldiers might actually go through with the crucifixion and the Master would die—a terrible suspicion that Jesus might have read the signs incorrectly, that Yahweh would not intervene and rescue him from the jaws of death. But there is no evidence to support it.

There has also been elaborate speculation that the Judean disciples, Joseph of Arimathea chief among them, were still acting under Jesus' direct instructions, and were preparing a drug which, when he drank of it on the cross would cause him to appear dead and give them the opportunity to rescue and revive him before death overtook him. Proponents of this idea cite as evidence the 'wine mingled with myrrh' or 'gall' or a sponge filled with vinegar which Mark and Matthew say was offered him. But it is not persuasive.

According to the fourth gospel, the only one of his male compatriots present at the crucifixion was the Beloved Disciple. But the versions of Jesus' final agony differ so greatly between the gospels that even that is difficult to credit.

All are agreed, however, that the women who had accompanied him on his travels stayed with him until the end. That his mother was among them is doubtful and the oblique references in the synoptics to her as 'the mother of James and Joses' are highly suspect. For if the Mary they allude to was, in fact, Jesus' mother there is no plausible reason for their not having called her so.

As Mark would have it, Jesus reached the place of execution just before the third hour of the Jewish day, at about 9 a.m., and almost immediately his agony on the cross began. The other synoptics follow the Marcan lead, though the fourth gospel claims the crucifixion took place at midday. The difference is significant in deciding which of the accounts is the more credible and in this instance, as in so many others, the Marcan version is considerably more convincing. For, weakened and infirm as Jesus may have been, crucifixion was never a quick death, its victims often lingering for two or three days, and the period which John assigns to Jesus' ordeal is suspiciously short.

Even the six-hour period asserted by Mark has caused orthodox scholars to pause. But then the orthodox vision of

Jesus the man has allowed for no blemish to mar the perfection of his earthly body, however irrelevant they might claim such considerations to be.

One cannot but feel that in the face of such terrible suffering quibbling of this kind is graceless. But however one might wish that it had never occurred, that the man might have been spared such pain, there can be no question that he took it upon himself—in pursuit of a strange, unhappy delusion perhaps, but he did it of his own will.

There can be little question, too, that his faith assured him that he would not die there, that this, the final gesture, would be the last key in the divine plan which would unlock the door to heaven—the New Kingdom.

It may have been that he relied on Psalm 138:

> Though I walk in the midst of trouble, thou dost preserve my life; thou dost stretch out thy hand against the wrath of my enemies, and thy right hand delivers me. The Lord will fulfil his purpose for me; thy steadfast love, O Lord, endures forever. Do not forsake the work of thy hands.

Indeed, he may have found his inspiration in a whole variety of sacred writings, for the Old Testament abounds in such imaginings.

As the hours passed, says Mark, passersby mocked and derided him calling, 'Save yourself! Come down from the cross!'[7] The felons crucified with him scorned and cursed him in their agony.

For once, Matthew finds no need to elaborate or to fulfil prophecy and remains faithful to the Marcan text until Jesus' death.

Luke is less restrained. The author has Jesus seeking forgiveness for the Roman soldiers who crucify him—'Father, forgive them; for they know not what they do'—and showing gratitude to one of the robbers who defends him from the jibes of the other—'Truly, I say to you, today you will be with me in Paradise'.[8]

In John he speaks with the Beloved Disciple, and directs his mother to live with the disciple. In this gospel, the robbers are silent.

All gospels are decidedly suspect. One can see and feel the clouds of myth and legend descending upon the scene ever more thickly, the eager imaginings of the gospel writers obscuring the truth with their mighty visions of a god.

A single cry breaks through. It is Jesus in his final agony and the cry pierces the heart of all within range of it: 'E'lo-i, E'lo-i, la'ma sabach-tha'ni?…My God, my God, why hast thou forsaken me!'[9]

It is the single most terrible and frightening cry in the history of man. It is the final despair. It is the sudden, awful realisation as the lifeblood departs that there is nothing to take its place; that it has all been for nought.

Orthodox scholars have tied reason in knots in their attempts to explain it away. It has been said, for instance, that he was merely beginning to recite Psalm 22 when death overwhelmed him. Others have claimed it as a mistaken interpolation; still others as a passing shadow of doubt.

If it had originated with Matthew or Luke there might be grounds for accepting it as an editorial addition designed to show a fulfilment of prophecy. But no amount of rationalisation can explain it away. It originated in Mark, the earliest and least corrupt of the gospels. And, as if to anticipate the squirming of the apologists, it is the only sentence from Jesus' mouth in the entire gospel which is rendered wholly in Hebrew before being translated into Greek, the language of the gospel writer. Its authenticity is rock solid.

Matthew repeats it (though he can hardly have appreciated its impact) probably because at the time of his writing Mark was well enough known for its absence to debase his credibility. The later writers, Luke and John, felt no such constraints. They expunged it utterly.

Too late, however, for its power to be dissipated; and 2,000 years after the cry reached the small group of women huddled at a distance from the cross, grieving for the one who had stood so vibrantly at the centre of their lives, it echoes still:

'My God, my God, why hast thou forsaken me?'

Notes

1. Mark 15:1.
2. Matthew 27:19.
3. Matthew 27:24-25.
4. Matthew 27:25-26.
5. Luke 23:3-12.
6. John 18:28-40; 19:1-16.
7. Mark 15:30
8. Luke 23:34 and 43.
9. Mark 15:34-35.

Epilogue

THE claim that Jesus was somehow resurrected has become the very essence of Christianity. No tenet of the faith is more stoutly defended, and rightly so, for if it did not happen as the churches claim, their very existence has been founded on a pathetic delusion, and the crimes against humanity which have been committed in the name of faith suddenly become stripped of their heavenly righteousness.

There is no intention in this present work to pursue the growth of the new cult which sprang up around the Galilean or to test in detail the various gospel versions of the 'resurrection'. But though they differ widely, the four gospels do contain elements in common, some of which are helpful in providing an outline of the events which followed Jesus' death.

According to Mark, Joseph of Arimathea learns of Jesus' death and hurries to Pilate with a request that he be allowed to take down the body for burial. Surprised at the speed with which the 'King of the Jews' had died, Pilate sends for the centurion in charge of the execution to be sure. The centurion reports that Jesus has in fact expired and Joseph is given the necessary permission.

Joseph hurries back to the hated Golgotha, takes down the body, wraps it in a linen shroud he has brought along for the purpose and places it in a nearby tomb 'which had been hewn out of the rock'. Then he rolls a stone against the entrance to the tomb. And, says Mark, Mary Magdalene and Mary the mother of Joses saw where he was laid.

Matthew paraphrases the Marcan text but then, unable to leave well enough alone, is constrained to add a paragraph designed to forestall the critics, or to answer a charge which was apparently common at the time of his writing. But as usual the author does more to harm his case than to help it.

'Next day,' he writes, 'that is, after the day of Preparation [the Sabbath itself] the chief priests and the Pharisees gathered before Pilate and said, "Sir, we remember how that imposter said, while he was still alive, 'After three days I will rise again'. Therefore, order the sepulchre to be made secure until the third day, *lest his disciples go and steal him away and tell the people, 'He has risen from the dead,'*(Italics mine) and the last fraud will be worse than the first." Pilate said to them, "You have a guard of soldiers; go, make it as secure as you can." So they went and made the sepulchre secure by sealing the stone and setting a guard.'[1] [Italics mine]

The author's intention is so transparently obvious that it needs no comment. The passage is interesting, however, in revealing the ignorance of the author with regard to Jewish custom. Only a poorly informed Gentile would suggest that the priests and Pharisees would engage in such business (or indeed business of any kind) on the Passover Sabbath. This alone is sufficient to put the passage quite beyond belief.[2]

Luke, once again, spurns the elaboration and contents himself with a paraphrasing of the Marcan narrative.

John's additions are only minor. Joseph of Arimathea is accompanied by Nicodemus in the quick burial ceremony and together the two men bind the body of Jesus in linen cloths together with 'about one hundred pounds' of myrrh and aloes and lay it in the tomb. Interestingly, he forgets to mention the sealing of the tomb with the stone at this point. It is only revealed as having been there two days later when it is rolled away.

It is this scene, in which the empty tomb is discovered, that marks the real beginning of a new religion. As such, it has been the subject of endless speculation and apology. For by now the narrative has almost ended and is being superseded by mystical visions and wishful imaginings. A world inhabited by human beings is in the process of replacement. Angelic figures reappear from the birth stories; the sun ceases to shine; temples tear themselves apart; the air is thick with portent.

Even Mark, the most reliable of the gospel writers, is infected by the feverish malady though, characteristically, he is much more restrained than his fellow biographers. He records that on the day after the Sabbath Mary Magdalene and Mary, the mother of James and Salome, bought spices that they might go and anoint him.

And very early on the first day of the week they went to the tomb when the sun had risen. And they were saying to one another, 'Who will roll away the stone for us from the door of the tomb?' And looking up, they saw that the stone was rolled back—it was very large. And entering the tomb, they saw a young man sitting on the right side, dressed in a white robe; and they were amazed. And he said to them, 'Do not be amazed; you seek Jesus of Nazareth, who was crucified. He has risen, he is not here; see the place where they laid him. But go, tell his disciples and Peter that he is going before you to Galilee; there you will see him, as he told you.' And they went out and fled from the tomb; for trembling and astonishment had come upon them; *and they said nothing to anyone, for they were afraid.*[3] [Italics mine]

Thus ends Mark.[4]

It is fitting that the most reliable of the gospels should end at that point, for what follows is a chronicle which by year and by century removes itself further and further from the central figure of Mark's story; the small, ungainly man driven by a need so terrible that he gave his life for it.

Soon, in the minds of men and women he would cease to be a figure of flesh and blood, of passions and lusts, of great strengths and crippling weaknesses. He would be deified in absentia; his strange, unnatural behaviour fitted only for the world of his fevered imagination—a world in which the rich and powerful are cast down and the poor and the crippled find perfect peace—would be codified and revered as 'righteousness', as appropriate human conduct. Then by fear and ruthless power, by fire and blood, it would be imposed and this act of imposition would itself become a virtue.

As it is today.

And everywhere the unnatural code would be broken and men would be riven by guilt, a force more terrible than any other. And everywhere that force would be employed to oppress the object of their guilt: the victims, the 'weaker' sex.

The rich and the powerful would inherit the earth…and they would preach in his name.

He sacrificed himself for this.

Notes

1. Matthew 27:62-66.
2. See p. 16.
3. Mark 16:1-8.
4. The best authorities bring the book to a close at the end of verse 8; in other versions, verses 9-20 follow immediately after verse 8.

Bibiliography

ALLEGRO, J., The Sacred Mushroom and the Cross, Hodder & Stoughton, London, 1970.

ALLEGRO, J., The Dead Sea Scrolls, Penguin, Harmondsworth, 1964.

BAUER, B., Criticism of the Gospel History of John and The Synoptics, 1840-42.

BRANDON, S.C.F., The Trial of Jesus of Nazareth, Batsford, London, 1968.

BULTMANN, R., Jesus and the Word, Scribner, New York, 1958. The History of the Synoptic Tradition, Oxford University Press, 1963.

CARMICHAEL, J., The Death of Jesus, Victor Gollancz, London, 1963.

DANIELOU, J., The Dead Sea Scrolls and Primitive Christianity, New American Library, New York, 1962.

DE CHARDIN, T., The Divine Milieu.

DIMONT, M.I., Jesus, God and History, New American Library, New York, 1962.

DURANT, W., Our Oriental Heritage, Simon and Schuster, New York, 1955.

EUSEBIUS OF CAESAREA, The History of the Church from Christ to Constantine (trans. G. A. Williamson) Penguin, Harmondsworth, 1965.

GIBBON, E., The Decline and Fall of the Roman Empire, Dent, London, 1957-60.

GLAZER, N.N., Jerusalem and Rome (The writings of Josephus), Fontana, London, 1966.

GRANT & FREEDMAN, The Secret Sayings of Jesus (Gospel of Thomas), Fontana, London, 1960.

JOSEPHUS., The Jewish War (Trans. G.A. Williamson, rev. M. Smallwood), Penguin, Harmondsworth, 1981.

KUNG, H., On Being a Christian, William Collins, London, 1977.

MACKEY, J.P., Jesus, the Man and the Myth, SCM, London, 1979.

MACKINNON, VIDLER, WILLIAMS and BAZZANT, Objections to Christian Belief, Pelican, Harmondsworth, 1967.

OLMSTEAD, A.T., Jesus in the Light of History, Scribner, New York, 1942.

PAGELS, E., The Gnostic Gospels, Weidenfeld & Nicholson, London, 1980.

POWELL DAVIES, A., The Meaning of the Dead Sea Scrolls, New American Library, New York, 1961.

REIMARUS, H.S., The Aims of Jesus and His Disciples, 1778.

RUSSELL, B., Why I Am Not a Christian, Allen and Unwin, London, 1957.

SCHONFIELD, H.J., The Authentic New Testament, Dennis Dobson, London,1956.

The Passover Plot, Hutchinson, London, 1965.

SCHWEITZER, A., The Quest for the Historical Jesus: A Critical Study of its progress from Reimarus to Wrede (trans. W. Montgomery), A&C Black, London, 1910.

SMITH, H. W., Man and His Gods, Little, Brown, Boston, 1952.

STRAUSS, D.F., The Life of Jesus Critically Examined, (trans. G. Eliot), Chapman, London, 1846.

SUETONIUS., The Twelve Caesars (trans. R. Graves), Penguin Books, Harmondsworth, 1957.

TACITUS., The Annals of Imperial Rome (trans M. Grant), Penguin, Harmondsworth, 1956.

TOYNBEE, A. (ed), The Crucible of Christianity, Thames &Hudson, London, 1962.

VERMES, G., The Dead Sea Scrolls in English, Penguin, Harmondsworth, 1962.

About the Author

ROBERT MACKLIN is one of Australia's most distinguished biographers and historians. His biography of Australian Prime Minister Kevin Rudd was a bestseller in Australia and China; he is the winner, with co-author Peter Thompson, of the prestigious 2009 Blake Dawson award for *The Big Fella – The Rise and Rise of BHP Billiton*. His 20 books include four novels, *The Queenslander, The Paper Castle, Fire in the Blood* and *Juryman*, adapted to the screen by MGM as *Storyville* starring James Spader and Jason Robards. But he is best known for his biographies of a wide range of Australian and international figures. *The Jesus Delusion* is the product of some seven years' research and writing. To view all Robert's titles visit www.robertmacklin.com

FEEDBACK & REVIEW
If you found this work engaging please write a review of it on Amazon. For your convenience, here is a link to the eBook on Amazon
To contact Robert about this book or to view his other titles, please visit www.robertmacklin.com or email him at robert@robertmacklin.com.

For eBook publishing, advice and marketing Robert chooses www.bwmbooks.com

Acknowledgements

I am happy to acknowledge the works of Bertrand Russell, Edward Gibbon, Will Durant and Flavius Josephus, whose books provided much of the basic intellectual framework for this present work.

They also provided that emotional sustenance during that difficult period of young manhood when the mental enslavement of 'faith' was overcome.